The Crossover

MAKING YOUR BIGGEST DREAMS YOUR GREATEST REALITY

JOSEPH G. SMITH, II

PUBLISHED BY FIDELI PUBLISHING INC. • WWW.FIDELIPUBLISHING.COM

© Copyright 2012, Joseph G. Smith, II

All Rights Reserved.

No part of this book may be reproduced, stored in a retrieval system, or transmitted by any means, electronic, mechanical, photocopying, recording, or otherwise, without written permission from the author.

ISBN: 978-1-60414-532-8

Joseph G. Smith, II
402.917.6679
GlobalRenaissanceMovement@Gmail.com
www.GlobalRenaissanceMovement.com

Published by Fideli Publishing Inc.
119 W. Morgan St.
Martinsville, IN 46151

www.FideliPublishing.com

Table of Contents

Prologue	The Omaha Ambassador Trek	vii
Chapter 1	**Participation**	1
	A Crossover Story: William Kampwamba	6
	A Crossover Story: Ashley Qualls	13
Chapter 2	**Respect**	17
	A Crossover Story: Arion Rashad	27
Chapter 3	**Optimism**	31
Chapter 4	**Growth**	39
	A Crossover Story: Farrah Gray, the Realionaire	45
Chapter 5	**Responsibility**	49
	A Crossover Story: Moses	54
Chapter 6	**Energy**	59
	A Crossover Story: Wilma Rudolph	66
Chapter 7	**Support**	69
	A Crossover Story: John H. Johnson	75
Chapter 8	**Spirituality**	81
	A Crossover Story: A Beautiful Tea Cup	88
	Dream Fulfillment Exercises	97
Bonus	**It's Never Too Late**	107
	A Crossover Story: Reanna Profit and the SPRANIMALS	113
	Why I Build	119

The Global Renaissance Movement	123
Epilogue The Arkansas Ambassador Trek	127
Thank Yous and Blessings	131
Biography	137
Glossary of Key Terms and Elements	141

Dedication

This book is dedicated to all the dreamers, all the true believers, all the doers of good who daily fights the good fight. Your final victory is coming. Don't stop fighting. Don't stop believing. God is making a way, no matter what the negative naysayers say. I'm praying for you and prayer changes things!

To the Reader

The purpose of this book is to help people, particularly young people, to recognize their own talents, genius, and abilities so that they may progress toward making the Great Crossover of bringing their God-given dreams into our experienced reality so we may leave lasting legacies of positive change in the wake of what are their lives. The Great Crossover is completion of the dream fulfillment process; of making ones dreams come true, crossing from the realm of intangibility to our physical realm of existence. This Great Crossover is the definitive action of an individual or society moving from grand imaginations to grand achievements, from great intentions to great actions and living the blessed results from those actions. You will be inspired to take massive positive action immediately upon completion of this book toward making your own unique ideas come alive for the benefit of yourself and the rest of the planet. The hope is that you become a more disciplined self with a solidified confidence and faith in your ideas and ability to accomplish great things.

PROLOGUE

The Omaha Ambassador Trek

What would you attempt to do if you knew you would not fail?
— Robert Schuller

Each of us has our own dreams, our own vision of what our ideal futures might be and Lord knows that on that path to the future you set out upon there will be many things thrown in your way. The devil is busy and he is real good at using what politicians call "the kitchen sink strategy." It will seem at times that no matter what you do, no matter how hard you try, something, anything, everything is out to get and stop you. Not anyone else, just you. And on these particular days it can seem as if all the forces that have massed against you, can't miss. It's as if every dart they throw not only hits you but pierces your heart, if even for a little bit. We all go through it. You can call it your personal trials or paying your dues, it doesn't matter what you call it but it's not until moments of extreme adversity that you find out just what you're made of, when you first discover what it takes, the level of dedication and steadfastness that's required to not only stay on the path you've chosen but to go all the way to the end, declare victory only to bring on the next challenge.

Everything we've ever done has led us to this very place in time we now stand. No matter how terrible, great, tragic or wonderful our pasts have been our futures remain undetermined. Our fates have not been written as we still have choices to make, relationships to establish, love to give and help to offer one another.

I am the leader of The Omaha Dream Team, an 18-member coalition of young entrepreneurs and youth all from Omaha, Nebraska and all dedicated to making a positive difference within our own community and in the world at large. Individually each member of our Omaha Dream Team are affiliated with a plethora of community and social organizations and churches and are all working to help young people and improve the quality of life in our local communities. We are business owners, educators, entrepreneurs, authors, students, fitness instructors, and international humanitarians and so much more. We are committed to and are taking righteous actions to do our part in positively advancing the plight of humanity and leaving our own unique legacy for the evolving history of humankind. We are leaders who yearn to show youth the path to personal achievement and success through love, service, and dedication to our brothers and sisters in our collective society.

We seek to complete the first Omaha Ambassador Trek, a coalition effort of Omaha, Nebraska entrepreneurs and youth working together in concert to implement the Ambassador Trek program of Non-Government Organization Build On; a historical first for our city and state. Our Omaha Dream Team of community leaders will spend 15 days living with host families in a Malawian village outside the capital city of Lilongwe during the initial construction phase of the building of our 3-room schoolhouse, a school in which 50% of the student body will be female thereby combating gender inequality. The Omaha Ambassador Trek is a real affirmation of our teams shared philosophy that when people can and have the ability to do something good for others then we should act and do those good deeds that we know must be done. The program description for the Omaha Ambassador Trek can be seen here: The program description for The Omaha Ambassador Trek can be seen here: http://webuildon.buildon.org/the-omaha-ambassador-trek/ and http://www.buildon.org/get-involved/build-a-school/

I'm not the only one here in Omaha with a vision, a passion for something more but it takes more than simply wishing for something good to happen to make it so. You have to get out there and cultivate the dream that you have as it first starts out like as a seed in your mind until one day when the vision is made real and you have demonstrated to the world your own level of greatness and ability. As I move forward on this project and work to make it real; to transition from the intangible to the physical there are doubts that the devil tries to put in my head but I know, within my soul that this is my destiny and will be done and will have a greater impact on our community than even I imagine. I just know it. When you have a passion and it's all that you think about and dream about, there comes a moment when all you can do is pursue it and nothing else; to do everything within your power to make others take up your dream as their own until one day your dream is no longer a dream but instead a real occurrence able to be felt and experienced by others. That is the path I'm on now. That is what this Omaha Ambassador Trek to Malawi, East Africa means to me and I want to say to you, the reader, that if you do not have a passion or a dream of this magnitude and as meaningful to you, please by all means borrow my dream. Take this dream of mine and run with it and help me to make this what it all can be.

Young people are historically charged to protect and guide the future. It's the youth who will discover the solutions to the problems that trouble us. Within us all are the seeds for personal achievement and intellectual ascendency. Human capital across the board must be protected and cultivated and shared not only for the continued improvement of our social order but to also prevent our own destruction. Those seeds of solutions must be cared for and offered the best that life has to offer so they may one day be employed to benefit the next generation as well as our own.

Our imaginations are our preview of the future. What as a community are we imagining? The media makes the choice to focus on the negative; the worst-case scenario that could possibly play out within the lives of Americans. As a team we imagine a unified city where all citizens are offered the maximum opportunities. Where children know no limits of their potential and discover their ability to achieve is in fact without bounds. A human beings potential to create the maximum amount of good for the most people in current existence is astronomical. Our abilities are as infinite as the ever expanding universe where we all now dwell yet cannot fully fathom.

I need The Omaha Ambassador Trek to become an amazing success for me as you need your dreams to become an amazing success for you. In the city of Omaha, Nebraska, the successful implementation of this endeavor will breathe life into my other programs and initiatives and serve as a blessed example of what can be done if youth have an idea that they love and believe in while maintaining the discipline required to see those dreams through to fruition. Discipline is doing what you're supposed to without anyone watching.

The motivations and reasoning behind The Omaha Dream Teams stewardship of The Omaha Ambassador Trek lie in our shared philosophical belief that each person has a responsibility to do what they can within their means to improve the plight of humankind. In our own unique and individual ways, we have a passionate desire to do something good for the less fortunate throughout the world while conveying the message to our youth that they have the power within themselves to change lives, heal a community and advance the planet. Throughout our individual and collective actions we work to have a greater impact within the lives of those who need our help and shape young minds with the knowledge and know-how to be more competitive on the world stage while assisting in the redevelopment of the United States. The Omaha Ambassador Trek will give participating youth the opportunity to get their passports and travel to another country, confront intense poverty and do something effective to combat it ... build a school!

If America is to be successful and get back on the path to prosperity our youth must understand and be engaged with the rest of humanity whom they might otherwise never encounter during the unfolding of broader human events. The Omaha Ambassador Trek contributes to this effort. The Omaha Ambassador Trek, by definition of the activities and actions involved will reveal to all participants that they have the power within themselves already to not just change their lives but to create the future and to do immense good. The development of the young people during the 15 day Omaha Ambassador Trek will result in a changed human being who will return to the Omaha community with their eyes wide open to some of the more perplexing realities facing humankind with a new confidence, experience and an amplified desire to be their best selves while working alongside others for the positive uplift of the human species. Alumni of the Omaha Ambassador Trek will become positive examples to their peers and leaders within the community and shining stars in the classrooms of the Omaha public school system.

To have the things we've never had before we've got to do the things we've never done before. I believe in God and believe that through him all things are possible and I believe that from this date of your reading my thoughts, a blessing, unknown to me at the time of this writing, will occur. Some people live their lives for a single moment. We live ours for all the moments that all of life has to offer. We aim to utilize the blessed gifts from the treasured past to impact the future long after we're gone. The young Malawian students who attend classes in the schoolhouse we build with your help, may very well go on and create the tools or offer the inspiration to avert disaster or exact Gods glorious wonders for the benefit of all.

As blessed as I am what I hope and desire most to achieve is to have a lasting legacy that will be appreciated but more importantly helpful to the future of humankind. I'm talking in terms of Imhotep, John Brown, Toussaint Loverture, Thurgood Marshall, King Menes, Martin Luther King Jr., and my Lord and Savior Jesus Christ.

I hope you appreciate and enjoy the work I have prepared and that the Lord blesses you as he has so certainly blessed me.

Peace and P.R.O.G.R.E.S.S.,

Joseph G. Smith, II

Schedule and Plans for the 1st Omaha Ambassador Trek

The specific activities to be completed throughout The Omaha Ambassador Trek includes and is not limited to social studies coursework and curriculum tie-ins. Participants will immerse themselves in and study things as:

- Nation building in the contemporary world; geopolitical, cultural, military, economic and international relationships.
- Recent African history: political divisions, systems, leaders, religious issues, resources and population trends.
- Life in a developing country; characteristics, challenges and future.
- Malawian literature and cultural exports.

Itinerary in Malawi

Day 1

Depart airport (overnight on plane)

Arrive in Lilongwe

Check-in at hotel

Make phone calls home

Overnight in hotel

Day 2

Breakfast in capital

Change money

Travel to BuildOn impact area

Lunch in town

Travel to village

Village orientation

Spend first night with host families

Day 3- 13

Ground breaking on schoolhouse construction site

Work on the construction of the schoolhouse

Live with host families

Daily culture and Education workshops

Daily group reflection, journaling, and enrichment activities

Field trip to other BuildOn built schools

Day 14

Leave village

Travel to capital

Overnight in capital hotel

Day 15

Cultural touring Final dinner

Depart capital

Arrive Home

Continue to change the world

For more information and to support The Omaha Ambassador Trek please visit **GlobalRenaissanceMovement.com** or contact **GlobalRenaissanceMovement@gmail.com**

BELIEVE ~ ACT ~ PERSEVERE ~ SUCCEED

IT'S POSSIBLE!

The Right idea is certain to fly!

*No matter what anyone says or even if it has never been done before!
Orville and Wilbur Wright were right!*

The Wright Brothers, Kitty Hawk, North Carolina 1903

CHAPTER 1

PARTICIPATION

I am sure in my own mind that the one business of life is to succeed, that God did not give us these magnificent brains, these miraculous personalities, and these wonderful physical qualities and then expect us to waste our lives in failure.

— **Sterling W. Sill**

At the time of this writing, I am 31 years young. As 2012 comes to a close and 2013 approaches, my dream, one of the many, is to have this book published. Good things come to those who wait this is true, but equally true is that great things happen when you go for it. That is my message to you, to GO FOR IT! Your dreams ... GO FOR IT! Your ideas ... GO FOR IT! Becoming a better you ... GO FOR IT! Being a better student ... GO FOR IT! Maximizing your talents ... GO FOR IT! Changing our world ... GO FOR IT!

One of the most important truths I can make known to you is that your ideas, plans, and dreams can come true and be made real. A new innovative, never having existed before product, service, business or social effort born of your own imagination is possible to make real, achieve and PROFIT from. This is a great truth because it is happening all the time but not happening nearly enough. With unprecedented access to the world's wealth of information and our near instantaneous global connectivity to one another there is no good reason that more of our young folk should not be social engineers, leaders, business partners and developers. No matter if your idea is a free method to improve a person's profile page on a social networking site or to create a comic book series of characters you dreamt of during random nights of slumber, those ideas and visions can in fact be brought to life, used and profited from for your benefit by you! People often say "It would be cool if they made _____." You can fill in the blank with whatever you imagine and while you are doing that I want you to realize that YOU can be THEY. That YOU have the power, intelligence, and ability to create what the world needs. Stop waiting for someone else to do what you have already thought of.

The statement "I'm going to start a business when I grow up" should no longer part from a young person's lips again. The time to start a business is the very moment they have the combined energies of an original idea and the courage to act boldly. I recognize that not everyone is going to start a business and not everyone is going to nor have the desire to invent anything. For those people who do other things in life and within our society; God bless you on your journey. We love you, we support you and we wish you all the best. But for some of us we have something that has been firmly placed within our hearts and we will never be satisfied or content to rest without achieving what we progressively become convinced is our designed purpose in this life. Your purpose, your dreams need not wait.

The contents herein are an offering of what I have come to know to be the key ingredients for success taken from my own experiences, lessons learned and examples available for both you and I to follow of those who have already done what we seek to do. The fact that these ideas and strategies worked and are available for your intellectual consumption in the time frame I've set out is all the proof I need that these strategies, methods and principals; the P.R.O.G.R.E.S.S. PRINCIPLE works and will work for you if passionately persistently applied.

You cannot win the game if you are not first in the game. You cannot conquer what you do not confront. You may have a vague and general interest in a particular subject, activity or something in which you lack any specific information. All you know is that you like participating in science projects or you really enjoy solving math problems, not because you really like it but because you like that you are so very good at it. You like the way you can solve algebraic equations in your head while everyone else must use whole oak trees of scratch paper only to get the wrong answer. Whatever interests you have, these are things that you can and should capitalize on.

The first plank of the success strategies I've created, that I have followed and what has worked for me in what I call The P.R.O.G.R.E.S.S. PRINCIPLE is so instrumental because there must be **PARTICIPATION** in the industry or field that has so fixed the gaze of your minds eye upon it. You like science experiments so you join the science club. You love chess so you join the chess team. Upon first suggestion someone may be inclined to make fun of another who joins the chess team but would you care about what other people thought if you found out that big league chess competitors earn over 100 grand per year doing what they grew up loving… PLAYING CHESS! It would not be wise to allow someone else's limited worldview to stop us from becoming all that we have within us to become. It's too easy for us to simply follow the script we were given. You know the one. The very script you or someone you know may be following now. It goes like this: *(See if you can get the answers correct as you read. They are placed at the bottom of the page if you need help. Feel free to write the answers in the blank space).*

A. Well, you're 5 years old. It's time for you to start going to
_____.

B. At school, follow instructions, study hard and get good
_____.

C. That way when you're 18 you can get accepted into the best
_____.

D. At college, study hard and keep getting really good
_____.

E. That way when you graduate you can get a good
_____.

F. Be honest, work hard and that job will take care of you for the rest of your _____.

G. Our society calls this living _____.

ANSWERS TO BASIC SCRIPT OF LIFE: Answers go in order from first blank space to last. **A.** School, **B.** Grades, **C.** College, **D.** Grades, **E.** Job, **F.** Life, **G.** The American Dream

You can tell the out datedness of the script we're given because that great job that society promises will be available upon your leaving school is no longer there. In our new globalized economy and predicted futures of economic uncertainty there is nothing that we really can count on other than our own creativity, ingenuity and internal drive to make things happen. This is why more and more people are becoming entrepreneurs, inventors of incredible systems and dreamers of the new ideas shaping our current realities. Mark

Zuckerburg, the facebook inventor created this revolutionary communications tool *BEFORE* he left college. He didn't go out and get a job, he created thousands of other jobs for other people all from the power of his own idea. Going to school and getting good grades are extremely important but we have to remember that we can do things our own way and have those ideas come to life and work for us and for other people as well. With all the resources you have available to you there is no need to wait!

Our biographies are being written each day by and of ourselves through each decision we make and by the actions we take and at the end, when our lives have run their course and are extinguished we leave nothing behind except the sum total of our actions, efforts and accomplishments. Our deeds done, no matter how foul or righteous will speak louder and longer than any well-written eulogy. It is our actions that will speak to those we leave behind and the generations yet to come. As time rolls by, faster and faster like it always does, the opportunity to do the good work we are capable of is either utilized for the betterment of our communities or wasted toward the concentration of things that are of no consequence. In the final analysis of our lives most things we have ever done matter not save for the good deeds done in the world. Certainly no greater good can be done than the work to uplift and enlighten others.

A CROSSOVER STORY

William Kampwamba

Not one person can save the world but everyone everywhere can, in some way, no matter how small make the days ahead better ones for someone else. It is the unique story of William Kampwamba, a young man from a small village in Malawi, which like many other villagers lived life without power, electric power that is. The desire to live a better life was there but the resources to create one were almost non-existent. After being forced out of school because he couldn't pay the tuition he spent his days at the library where he came across a book about windmills and how to make them. He took it home, read the book and immediately went to work applying the knowledge he gained from the book. The book he just happened to stumble across taught him how to use trash from a landfill to build a windmill capable of generating enough electricity to give power to over a dozen homes for the first time ever. Using only discarded bicycle parts, plastic pipes, tractor fans and car batteries he did what others said could not be done as they laughed at his attempt. He wasn't afraid and he wasn't deterred and everyone reaped the rewards of his hard work and dedication.

The people of Williams's village did not know what he was doing. Some people actually thought he was going crazy but like most great thinkers and achievers of the past there was a method to what appeared to be madness. He believed in himself, <u>his</u> ideas and ability as you must believe in your ideas, ability and believe in your methods no matter if others perceive it to be madness. *"My dream is to finish my education and start my own company about the windmills. Most people they want technology but they cannot use the internet technology without electricity. That's what I'm planning to do is develop reliable electricity. Yeah, that's what I'm planning to do".*

Thinking about this story you might assume correctly that it was the book he found that led to this young man's ability to create such a power structure and while this assumption may very well be correct you would be leaving out a very critical element that makes this incredible story what it is. It was this man's powerfully passionate persistence in pursuit of transforming his life and the lives of his countrymen that really allowed for the miracle to occur. It is his passionate persistence that is to be credited with the results. After all, if he were not self motivated to pick up the book, read it and apply the knowledge there never would have been a story to be told. In that small part of Malawi, the lights might still be out.

We each have whatever resources life has allotted us. What we do with those resources is up to us. If we sit around, pout, complain and whine about what we don't have or if we take whatever meager resources available to us in our local landfill and build an electric power source, is also up to us. What do we do moving forward as we come across obstacles big or small? How can we begin with the territory/resources that we have now in our possession and expand upon them and shape them into a more blessed and bountiful future for not only ourselves but for others? We must do two very important things: first BELIEVE and second TAKE MASSIVE ACTION.

We have to take massive action because the challenges we face are massive and consequences of our inaction will be massive unless we keep moving forward. No matter how many hits we take, no matter how often or how hard the negative forces in life knock us down we must keep moving forward. We must not quit. To do so would be to become the walking dead. Not a zombie but a person physically alive but mentally and spiritually dead. Walking, talking and moving about through life but aimlessly and without purpose. We were born for and meant to do more than simply exist. It is our historical obligation to humanity that we do all that is possible for the positive advancement of the whole human race lest we descend into a lower state of relations with one another and lose what it is that makes us human to start; our connection to and love for one another. We all are the children of God and as we work to enhance the illuminating abilities of others we also do the same for ourselves. I firmly believe that we should not be competing with one another but rather completing one another. Something we must come to learn is that when we help enough people get what they want, we can have everything that we want. Wanting what we want is perfectly fine. This is just our natural self-interest. Self-interest is also perfectly fine as long as we do it in a positive way. We each are a fraction of the whole that is humanity.

What are you waiting for?

Action is the foundational key to all success.

—Tony Robbins

Nothing can take the place of or equal in value the wisdom one gains from their elders. But not just any elder, one who has lived a life of dedication to something beyond themselves; bringing out the greatness within others and creating a more equalitarian society for the benefit of all. I had the opportunity to visit with such a person recently and walked away motivated and inspired on a level not felt for some time. I was asked a question that is relevant to many of us at many times in our lives in relation to our dreams, goals and greater ambitions.

Surely there is something we all want, something that we desire on a deeper level that we feel that if this thing is acquired or task achieved it would bring about great levels of joy and give our lives some special meaning. This thing that we want at times we feel like we can't seek out until certain conditions have first been met. Sometimes we can get so wrapped up in preparing for fear of failing or avoiding embarrassment that we can delay ourselves to the point of total stagnation. Preparation and proper planning are not just good things they are also required things if we are to have the success we so desire. But there comes a point when we go from planning to fearing, fearing rejection or the negative opinion of the many haters out there. You can't plan for a perfection that cannot be attained. Just get started!

Fear is not all bad. A healthy dose of fear can keep you alert and alive but we should never allow it to cause goal-oriented paralysis. We must not allow the untold unknowns keep us from showing others what is known and that is that we are all endowed with the ability to create great things and reach our own levels of greatness. My elder, my new friend whom blessed me with majestic inspiration asked me as I ran down a list of things I had yet needed, "what are you waiting for"?

Witnessing the passionate fire in her eyes while hearing those words "what are you waiting for?" was the catalyst for change I needed at that moment. Sometimes in the midst of our optimism seeds of doubt can take hold and should that happen we must feel the fear and do it anyway. We've got to take that chance and pursue the opportunity as if our lives depend upon it because they do. We hear people say it and we know that we should do it, but stepping out on faith is hard because of its natural intangibility. Believing without proof, stepping forward with no knowledge of solid ground ahead is difficult but essential for us to get to where we've never been but know within our hearts we must be.

One of my favorite hip-hip artists is New York based rapper Common. His 2007 single "The people" is really good music and inspiring like most of his work but it is this song that offers a pointed message of how to proceed on our path. In the song he raps, *"Nobody believes, until I believe me. Now I'm on the rise doing business with my guys. Visions realized, music affecting lives, a gift from the skies to be recognized. I'm keeping my eyes on the people that's the prize."*

Who are the people? The people are all of us but specifically they are those who have been marginalized, forgotten about, abused, oppressed, those who suffer silently, those who suffer loudly but whose cry we've turned a deaf ear to. There are always obstacles and challenges in the battle between optimism and pessimism that forever rages but we live now at a time when one might think pessimism could become the victor of the two forces. We hear all the time about a new poll suggesting that America is not headed in the right direction or that the state of global affairs is one of tremendous bleakness, but for the people of that belief I say to you that the best way for us to predict the future is to create it ourselves. If you do not like the world that you were born into, if you do not like the world that your children will one day inherit then the decision must be made to change it, to correct it, to right the wrongs that have been left idle for so long. Things are not the way they are but rather the way we allow them to be. Our collective human condition has been longing for the genuine careful love of individuals devoted toward the positive advancement of us all.

It has been said that our net worth can be determined or summed up by the net worth of our five closest friends. The accuracy of such a measuring varies with each person and circumstance yet there is truth in it as to some degree we are a composite of our chosen surroundings. If those you hang out with on a regular basis are negative, disruptive and mean spirited people than the likelihood of you becoming negative, disruptive and mean spirited increases and vice versa if those whom you call friends are typically engaged in educational advancement, are seeking enlightenment and wealth building don't be surprised if that is what you're tracking towards as well. In the proverbial case of "who you know" it is not either/or but rather both /and. It is about WHO we know but it is also about WHAT we know. The combined strength of these two factors leads to success in business, product creation, college placement and dream fulfillment. You cannot afford to live another day without at least trying to get near to all the big small things that are the prerequisite for dream fulfillment. No game can be won without your competing in it.

Do not take the fact that you like or are good at something lightly. Anything that you have a natural liking for is something you will devote your passionate attention towards. Anything you are good at can certainly be capitalized upon especially when combined with the natural passion that comes with being proficient in some area. Being great or the best at something turns us on! It activates all our brain cells. It swells the ego. It clears the mind and instills courage within our hearts. But you've got to be engaged. You've got to be aware.

You have to be motivated and you've got to be active. Some of us are self-motivated. I'm self-motivated. We know what we want and know that we'll get it even without knowing how, so we go after it day after day in spite of failure and setbacks. Sure we get discouraged and upset and though we may be discouraged, we are not defeated. We are not deterred. While our personalities exhibit these characteristics, others need stronger doses of outside encouragement and support. We must seek out others with like-minded interests to offer us what we do not have ourselves. Learning from our elders and those with greater experience is a blessed opportunity that we should seek as often as possible. Few resources are on par with the wisdom and knowledge of those who have already ran the race we have only just begun.

Let us decide today to do what should have been done but wasn't. Let us decide today to live the way we must and care in ways we are capable for the mutual blessing of all of our families of every person in every land. Let us go forth to lead the land we love, asking his blessing and his help, but knowing that here on Earth God's work must truly be made our own.

A CROSSOVER STORY

Ashley Qualls & Whateverlife.com

Successful people do what failures don't!

—Tony Robbins

The resources you need to start a business and make your dream come to life are all around you. Facebook, the creation of a college kid, is a global phenomenon but before Facebook became king all my friends and I had a myspace page. That and a Black planet account. My Space was all the rage at the start of the new millennium. Everyone created their own personal space online to share music, photos and swap stories, express themselves in new and exciting ways and while most were creating a profile to look at, Ashley Qualls was thinking of a creative method of improving the myspace experience. Ashley Qualls looked at her digital surroundings, saw what was missing and proceeded to go about the task of creating a new and free service of personalizing someone's Myspace page. Crazy about dolphins? How about a background of dolphins doing back flips through hoops of fire? In love with the moon, stars and the rest of the cosmos? Whateverlife.com can/will create for you the background image you've only dreamt of.

As early as 9 years old, as a hobby, she began just playing around in web design from her family's old computer. When Ashley wasn't playing games as all kids do at that age, she did what most others didn't; she taught her herself useful skills like the basics of web design. At the youthful age of only 14 Ms. Qualls completed the first step in an online venture, which is to purchase a domain name. It may appear to others that by sheer coincidence the concept of WhaeverLife.com came about but I do not believe that. I don't believe in coincidences. I believe that things happen for specific reasons to keep us from harm or to help usher us into our destinies. In my view this was the case for Ashley when after losing a video game to a friend, she dropped the controller and blurted out, "Whatever, Life." She liked it instantly and immediately thought it to be the great name of a website. What happened for Ashley in this moment was more than chance blurting out of a random statement. What happened was Ashley had an EPIPHANY! Upon uttering the words after dropping the controller, she knew right away what this was, a great idea. She didn't need to think about it. She didn't need to sleep on it. She knew! She trusted her gut instincts in that moment and recognized this epiphany for what it was, a sudden realization of great truth!

She had been playing around with her design work that sparked interest in only her circle of friends at first until she figured out how to customize MySpace pages. After that, history took over as at first several of her classmates asked her to design their sites and dozens more. Things began to grow after that when she connected with Google AdSense, a service that supplies advertisements to a website and shares the revenue with the owner of that site (A great resource for you if you have an online presence as I do).

Whateverlife.com attracts millions of visitors and page views per month generating millions of dollars in advertising revenue. With as many young people there are spending time decorating their social networking profile pages and making slide shows, Ashley Qualls used her natural born talents and skills she learned to facilitate this online revolution. When she first got started no one would have guessed that she would have went from basic online doodling to a multifaceted tech company offering more than just MySpace layouts but also cell phone wall paper, an online magazine and more. In Ashley's home office she works doing only what she has loved to do since she was 9 years old and in doing so has brought in as much as $70,000 per month!

Ashley Qualls made over a million dollars through the sale of advertisements on her website. She did what I'm suggesting that you do, create something that the world needs or wants. Look at your world. What is something that would make life better, more convenient and give us less hassle? Think of that thing and invent that thing. Create that thing. Use that thing to shape the future and rebuild the world. Ashley Qualls took that million dollars and bought her mom a new house as well as launching more programs and business initiatives. You can do the same thing! You could be more focused on the Kardashians and who they plan to soon divorce, but why? With all the money out there to be made I figure you would be better served building your brand and selling your service and cashing checks from your own hard work. I'm not saying that money is the most important thing, but it ranks right up there with Oxygen!

Successful people do what failures don't!

— Tony Robbins

CHAPTER 2

RESPECT

*Success is a process, not an event.
It is a journey not a destination*

— Zig Zigler

You must give respect to get respect. Respect for others, respect for yourself, and respect for the process. **RESPECT** for your own personal progress. Nothing happens overnight. Sure the Powerball lottery could, potentially happen overnight but the odds of such a fortunate occurrence are 1: 195,249,054. It's unwise to count on that to be your safety net or bearer of fortunate financial fruit. There are many must-dos to be checked off the list before you reach a magnificent moment of self-actualization but primarily is respect for oneself. You must respect yourself!

Part of respecting yourself is to know your worth. Do you know how much your individual self is worth? You are priceless. You are beyond the assignment of money in any amount. You are a marvelous work of art born of Gods imagination. You are priceless for reasons not short of your unique personhood but you do have a monetary value placed on your life attributable to your talents, skill sets, abilities and your level of willingness to work hard for what you want. The sum total of all this is your *human capital*, the amount of information, knowledge and skills one is able to bring to bear to solve problems and advance the world, which is in fact our true purpose.

Respecting yourself begins with treating yourself well. Treating yourself as you would have others treat you. You must walk, act, and treat yourself with dignity at all times. You must carry yourself as if you were worthy of the respect of others because you are! Young ladies must know that no one will hold them in a higher regard than themselves. Our young men must know that to resist the urgent impulses of the moment is to avoid danger as well as to enhance their own personal value. The decisions we make are our own and the benefits and consequences of our actions will be felt by us, and oftentimes, those we love most. Therefore, we must be careful in the steps we take and the actions we make. Eating healthy and maintaining a healthy lifestyle is a choice the same as using drugs and dropping out of school is a choice. Sure, it's best to be healthy and drug free but the choice is ours alone to make. Which choice do you believe will offer you the opportunity for the advancement of your dreams?

Taking care of yourself and being mindful of what you do with or put in your body is important but an important element of respecting oneself is to respect your intellectual/physical/social potential. One of the greatest forms of self-respect is to always maintain, increase and market your human capital. Knowledge is the currency of our times. The more you know the more you will grow and the more you grow the farther you can go. This is truer than most people realize. It's never really too late to start your journey of dream fulfillment as long as you're alive but you can absolutely prolong your own agony and delay deserved rewards by passing up opportunities to advance, grow and evolve into a more intelligent human being.

Only you can decide what you are going to do. Go to college or not? Start a business or not? Regularly take in information that will aide in your growth as a person and allow you to better master and market your own talents or don't? You could choose to remain as you are, where you are, complacent and oblivious to the wonders of life and the wondrous things that could be done by you for others or you can choose to break through your own barriers and put an end to your own inertia.

This is something that must be done but is not easy. This is about more than just staying in school. Staying in school is certainly a good thing and I encourage you to pursue your schooling with great enthusiasm as knowledge is power, but lots and lots of people are staying in school, graduating and going on to live very mediocre lives. Some people graduate, think of an original idea and master a skill set then go on to change the world. What's the difference between the two groups? I want you to challenge yourself to becoming the best you possibly can, to become extraordinary; to put these extraordinary talents of yours to work.

History has been changed for the better by many people from many different backgrounds but the traits of these remarkable individuals are all the same. They have not just an idea, not just some skill set they are proficient at and not just an education — all great and important prerequisites for success — but they had something more. They had passion. They had vision. They had drive. They had the capacity to passionately persevere in pursing that which made their hearts most happy.

Most of us have a mindset that we are our past. Many people can't ever get over the mistakes and failures of their past to transform themselves into better versions of who they used to be. Failure is part of success as failure is part of the process of growth and intellectual and professional development. If you can't move past your failures it's because you think that your biography equals your destiny, that the past equals the future. And, of course, it does if you live there. But we have to throw off this mindset that has been forced upon us which is poison. And if you think you can't overcome your mistakes and you can't be more than you are, then you have been infected by the poison. But you're a smart person and you know that a person can in fact move beyond their mistakes and stage a life comeback. This same ability applies to not just people but also nations. We need only look back in history to see how all nations at some point eventually saw the error of their ways no matter how painful that sight may have come about but the possibility of correcting ones mistakes does exist. Attempting a global takeover during the early 20th century was awful and evil from all points of view but during the terrifying times of World War II I'm sure there was hardly a soul living who would have guessed that today, some 70+ years later Germany and Japan would be two of the greatest allies of these United States in our modern times.

All this great and miraculous change is possible and inevitable in fact if we keep working toward it but the process of getting there has to be respected. If not, frustration will grip your mind and thwart your efforts. To make that great impact, to create a legacy worthy of remembrance in times far off you must believe when things are bad; really bad. You have to believe you can win even when everything says you can't and you won't; the tough turbulent times when you become almost convinced of your certain failure. That time is marked by moments when we say, "I'll never accomplish..." It's like being trapped in the desert dying, panting, needing and praying for water. And in chasing a mirage would you rather die seeking water with a possibility of having never found it or to exist and still die in the current position believing it was never real? Dying doesn't necessarily denote physical death but the slow agonizing death of a once promised future that needed only the nurturing goodness of positive action. I'm yet a young man but I can imagine the deep sorrow and regret of those who've lived life having never truly lived it. Surly the wealthiest place on earth is the cemetery. There you will find those who took with them to their crypts songs left unsung, pictures never drawn placed on the wall and hung, books that were never written and people who had yet been forgiven, dreams lost forever to fear; **F**alse **E**vidence **A**ppearing **R**eal. You must act! A choice must be made and you must decide how bad do you want it.

The more we learn the more enlightened people we become so that we may pass this knowledge to the generation that is coming up after us. It's easy to offer your opinion or advice to others. Those opinions come from our unique experiences but also just kind of what we've picked up from places that have formed our general thoughts about things. I believe in the thoughts, philosophies, ideas contained in this book. Everything in here is based upon my own life and experiences as I've tried to achieve greatness in my life. Now I have known success many times over in my life. I've achieved some pretty great things. I am happy to have done what I've done, graduating from college, co-authoring a book, and now spearheading Ambassador Trek programs in Arkansas and Nebraska where youth will have the opportunity to build a 3 room schoolhouse in Malawi, East Africa and Nicaragua, Central America. These are great things yet I am unsatisfied. These are terrific things yet I am unfulfilled.

I want and demand greater things from this life in this world and so should you. Even at this very moment as pen massages paper to bring you the physical manifestation of my thoughts, this book *The Crossover: Making Your Biggest Dreams Your Greatest Reality* is yet a dream. It is a dream of my own to have a completed project of my own generating large quantities of financial fruit. I want to get paid! There is no shame and nothing wrong with wanting money. The problem starts when we begin to value money over the lives of others. We can pursue profits but not at the expense of other people. **PEOPLE BEFORE PROFITS!** Always remember that. If you have never heard of the golden rule here it is: *Treat others as you would have* *them treat you.* Believe that the more we do this as a human family the greater peace and happiness we will all see and all feel.

While going after your dreams it is certain you will meet discouragement, rejection, failure, disappointment, grief and pain as you go forth happily to deal and dance with our most hated intangible enemies to advance progress toward the glorious future we envision. A price must be paid for you to make the great crossover, to bring forth the vision that has held the attention of your minds eye for so long. And if you dare not just to dream but to dream larger than your imagination has done before and willingly pay any price and bear any burden, having courageously done so you will cross that great divide, the abyss separating mediocrity and greatness, dreams and reality. Certainly with your tenacious effort, the grace of God will take you farther than you ever thought possible and with his holy help it shall be so.

The Beautiful Struggle

Security is mostly a superstition. It does not exist in nature, nor do the children of men as a whole experience it. Avoiding danger is no safer in the long run than outright exposure. Life is either a daring adventure, or nothing. To keep our faces toward change and behave like free spirits in the presence of fate is strength undefeatable.

—Helen Keller

Perhaps the most potent weapon people have at their disposal is the internal fortitude, strength and will to carry on through setback, heartache and the errors resulting from our trials. We all have our own cross to carry. Until we get to "the top" or make our way to our destinies, we must go through the intense rigors of trying to make "it" happen, whatever "it" is and however long "it" takes. Dream pursuit is difficult because it is a struggle like none other. The great crossover is not impossible to achieve but believing in the possibility of your victory is one of the hardest battles we will ever fight. Surely the one thing to accompany us along our arduous journey is doubt and for us to succeed, it must fail. It, doubt, must be overcome before we can ever achieve any physical victories.

The beautiful struggle, though beautiful is a struggle none the less and that means, to exert great pressure, energy and resources so that ones efforts bear fruit or problems become solved. No crop can be harvested without first sowing seeds and tending the fields and likewise no goal can be reached without first giving birth to an original idea and nurturing it through righteous action and adhering to your plans in spite of setbacks, deterrents, and especially all the comments from the negative naysayers, some of whom will be your friends and even members of your own family. In many respects, that is indeed the most difficult challenge; to overcome the odds on your at times perilous journey receiving from those who should be first to offer encouragement but offer instead scorn, criticisms and condemnation of your dreams. What amounts to dreams and/or fantasies of possible realities to others have become your entire life. How do you overcome the rejection of those you love most, who would benefit most from your achievements but offer vitriolic rhetoric instead? The answer to this lies within our own hearts and it is there we will find the strength, desire and will to succeed.

The struggle for your dreams begins and ends with you. No matter your desires and no matter the number or type of obstacle, success ultimately rests upon you. All struggles, great and small do come to an end but it is we alone who decide the circumstances of our fate. Victory or loss, success or failure ultimately depends upon you. What is the worth of your dreams to you? What are you willing to tolerate?

What burdens will you bear to bring about the great conclusion to your struggle? What are you willing to sacrifice to get the things that you want, please remember that to sacrifice means to give something up. What are you willing to give up for the things that you want? The struggle for our dreams can be a beautiful experience if and only if the intensity of that which opposes us is met by the greater ferocity for victory within our own hearts and our character through which we will ultimately persevere. Perseverance is possible but certainly not easy. To persevere means to endure. It means to walk upon the proverbial fork in the road and blaze a new trail through the middle as did the great pioneers of old. For what we choose to accomplish is a first, if not for humanity most assuredly for ourselves.

The end of that which we seek to accomplish will come into being when we realize that our purpose is stronger than the obstacles that attempt to thwart us, that our God given gifts, the unique talents that we possess and wield, are more potent than any weapon that can be drawn against us. Which is the reason why those weapons shall not prosper. While we are in it, our struggles do not seem beautiful at all. That is because our perspective on life and our status within it is skewed by the circumstances of the moment. We become so bogged down with our own tribulations that we fail to realize that we're being molded into better people by the pressures of the day. Your car breaks down and you must walk to your destinations for a time. It's tiring and you're hot and fatigued but until this moment you never knew how strong you were. Until that moment you never appreciated your vehicle the way you do now that it's gone. Until that moment you never knew empathy for those walking on the side of the road who you only thought of in anger as you perceived them to be in your way as you drove around in a needless hurry. The struggle, as difficult as it may have been and as long lasting as it may seem, only the struggle we're mired in is capable of making us into who we are destined to become.

The struggle is beautiful because it is existence within the struggle that we learn and come to know that we are more than soft bodies and minds easily susceptible to suggestions, it is only through the struggle we prove to others and ourselves that we are made of sterner stuff. We are capable of more than we know and we are powerful beyond measure. While we may not know how the struggle ends we do know that we have survived other struggles in our past and we will survive this one. We have succeeded in other areas and we will succeed in this one.

Throughout history it has occurred time and again that those who achieved greatness did so only while and after they were surrounded by what appeared to be total imminent defeat. As it was for histories heroes so it is for we trailblazers in our time carving a greater existence from remnants of eras gone by for the favored futures of sons and daughters who are themselves the mothers and fathers of our collective fortunes.

Galileo may have been convicted of heresy by the Catholic Church in 1633 but he did go on to invent the telescope, becoming an integral part of human space exploration. Thomas Edison failed many times to achieve the results he sought but said *"I have not failed. I've just found 10,000 ways that won't work."* He continues on to create one of humanities greatest modern marvels, commercially available electric light and with the phonograph...recorded sound! Having been turned down by over 1000 agents, becoming totally broke, divorced by his wife, even after going without heat in the harsh New York winter and turning down large sums of money offered and not as a reward for talents possessed or services rendered, Sylvester Stallone stood by his beliefs until he was offered what he sought all along, the leading role in the American movie classic "Rocky" and $35,000 cash. It wasn't the money he was after but the role in the film that he knew he was meant to play. This is a struggle we can recognize as a beautiful transition of one man with a dream into what and who we know as historic American heroes as Rocky

Balboa, John Rambo, and any given named mercenary for hire in the latest action flick coming to a movie theatre near you.

Your dreams are dreams until you and only you make them come true. Until you complete the great crossover, the completion of the dream fulfillment process, the journey of your dreams from the realm of thought and imagination to our experienced reality. This great crossover is not just possible it is inevitable so long as we never put to rest our desires for grand achievements offering our lives special meaning and likewise the world special gifts.

The dawning of a new world starts first with the dawning of a new self. That brilliantly radiant dawn is on its way, indeed it is on the horizon no matter how dim present surroundings may appear. Through faith, a terrific tenacious stick-to-it-tive effort, the blessings meant for you will arrive and with your ascention to greatness so too will you go on to bless others through righteous actions born out of brotherly love. Surely service is the rent that we pay to occupy our place in this time on this planet. *For someone, the light at the end of the tunnel is YOU!*

The struggle always continues as we always are evolving. History proves that if we remain steadfast and confident we will be victorious if we are forever forward moving. We cannot conquer what we do not confront so it is with hearts, souls and minds lit aflame with blessed enthusiasm for finer futures we charge, engage, and fight the good fight because we know we shall overcome!

A CROSSOVER STORY

Arion Rashad

Many of life's failures are people who did not realize how close they were to success when they gave up.

— Thomas Edison

I think it's interesting to come across amazing individuals who do amazing things at unexpected times and who really do come out of nowhere with it. Time and time again I'm confronted by stories of people who prove over and over again that any idea, any business, any transformative thought can be brought from the depths of our minds into the real for all the world to enjoy. That's how I feel and what I think about when I think of the story of Arion Rashad, who created and now markets and sells his own comic books called MII Toons at the tender age of 12! This young entrepreneur is already on his way to mega success as you can purchase his comic in stores now. A store employee of Tates comics, the store that gave this young businessman his big break said *"I've never heard of anyone 12, doing a comic. For somebody so young to put a book out, something so good, it's never been done. There's a lot of character development in it and a lot of subplots that he's got building up. At the end of #106 he's got a cliffhanger in there and I'm waiting for the next one [issue] to come out."*

This story is impressive on many levels for many reasons because the man is so very young and to have done what he did really is amazing. You can't look at this young man, learn his story and not stand in astonishment at what he's achieved. It really does cause a mind to ponder, how do I make MY dream come alive? How is it that he has done what he's done? Yet I have not done what I've wanted to do? Depending upon your personal outlook on life and your individual levels of optimism vs. pessimism you are either inspired by the story and want to create your own successes or you look at it as a great and amazing event but as something that you yourself cannot achieve on your own. Some people have this type of thinking that says "yeah, that's great what he did but I could never achieve something like that. Sure, it's wonderful a 12 year old boy invents his own comics and sells them to stores but I don't have any breaks like that coming my way." If this is how you are thinking, STOP IT NOW! We must not allow dark negative thoughts to infiltrate our inspiration and stop us from doing what we were born to do yet have not.

The whole wide world needs what you've got. The whole wide world needs your talents, needs your genius, needs your creativity, needs our humor, needs your inventions, needs your wisdom, needs your music, NEEDS YOU! What would the world be today if all the greats of the past never did what they did, never enacted their visions and went at the hard and gritty work of goal attainment and dream fulfillment? The very real truth is that there is no time to waste, not a second to spare as the days of our lives are coming to a close and before they do we must make maximum use of each breath in our lungs if we are ever to become what we know we are inside and do what we know we must. Arion took the time, talent and patience to apply those terrific tools to his vision and thus MII Toons was born. What is it that sits idle in the purgatory of your brain awaiting only your persistent action so that it, like all great creations of the past may make the great crossover and step into the real and breath life? A lovely lasting legacy, don't you think you should leave one? I do!

To subscribe to MiiToons or for more information visit www.miitoons.com or email Arion Rashad at info@miitoons.com

The credit belongs to the man who is actually in the arena. Whose face is marred by sweat and blood who strives valiantly, who errs and comes short again and again, because there is no effort without error and shortcoming, who knows the great enthusiasm, the great devotion, spends himself in a worthy cause, who best knows in the end the triumph of high achievement, who at worse, if he fails, at least fails while daring greatly.

— *Theodore Roosevelt 1913*

CHAPTER 3

OPTIMISM

I am an optimist. It does not seem too much use being anything else.

— Winston Churchill

We are living in extraordinary times. The global economic crisis has affected every nation on earth and just about everyone from we, the average citizen to big business to whole countries are doing some belt tightening. The near collapse of the financial system has sent more than shockwaves through the hearts and pocketbooks of everyone forcing us to reprioritize just about everything from what warrants a budget increase and if something needs simply to be cut. Certainly everything is up for discussion these days as we all, no matter of political affiliation are in need of solutions. Not a band-aid or some other cosmetic fix that will allow for the passage of our problems from this generation to the next but whole body reconstructive surgery. The challenges we face are unique and enormous and so the solutions to these problems must correspondingly be unique, enormous and smart. And we need unique and enormously smart people dedicated to inventing these solutions; for the solutions to our challenges will come from an enlightened human mind and that mind will not always belong to an American.

As we are all the children of God, so it is he who has blessed every man and every woman in every nation with the gifts of creativity and ingenuity. It is because of each of our incredible abilities that I've never been more optimistic about where we are headed as a country and global society. It truly is a great time to be an American.

You may not have heard that phrase written so brazenly as of late because of the myriad of woes permeating within our border. But I for one see not just opportunity but prosperity for our country and all others as our fates are joined and intertwined even more than our global economies. Perhaps the best example of this can be seen with the expanded immigration of Middle Easters to Detroit, Michigan and its surrounding areas. A snapshot of what's going on in America could be taken in Detroit. Perhaps no other city tells as much of what America is all about. The motor city as its still called in spite of huge job losses and closings of automotive plants, speaks to the city's people and their ability to create, innovate and draw a new future out of the remnants of eras gone by. This is the home of Motown, Ford and GM. And while this seemingly model of old time economic growth is confronting its issues, the people emigrating to the city have brought with them more than a desire to live a better life than in their native lands. They bring with them a resourcefulness, a beautiful sense of urgency that when combined makes for an orchestrated crescendo of economic growth, of boisterous brain activity capable of regenerating a city, able to revitalize the world's greatest democracy, gifting all of us with a planetary renaissance.

We are not diametrically opposed, you and I, us and them, Christians and Muslims, Americans and everyone else. What I and the rest of the Omaha Dream Team seek to do in building a school in Malawi is grand and ordinary, wondrous and normal. It's grand and wondrous because of what this is. It's ordinary and normal because of what this is. The building of a school truly is remarkable but we all have the power within ourselves to do it or something like it or even more prodigious. We need only to muscle up the gumption to start and have at it until the very end. I read somewhere once that if we'd only have faith as small as a mustard seed we'd soon realize our ability to move mountains.

In a November 2010 issue of Time magazine one of Detroit's economic engines many moving parts, Sami, an unemployed Iraqi refugee speaks without worry of not having a job because he knows it's only a matter of time that a local restaurant needs a busboy or something. At that point "I will save up for a couple of years and open a kebab shop ... then another and another one. If McDonalds can have restaurants all over the Arab world then why can't I have kebab shops all over America"?

It is Sami's unabashed **OPTIMISM** and his sense of purpose that we too must see within ourselves and exercise for our own advantage as well as the advancement of others. A school built for others is a blessing for the recipients as much as it is also for its builders. The illumination of knowledge burns brighter within the eyes of its beholder when coupled with the love for a brother or a sister. For as sure as the Omaha Dream Team has the same unabashed optimism and sense of purpose as Sami, we too will see to fruition our collective dream of offering the world what it needs more of...educated people. If Oprah Winfrey can build a school in South Africa, we can build a school in Malawi. The minds nurtured in our school will go on to become the economic engine parts of economies near and far with their own creative innovations. Their so doing will be grand

and ordinary, wondrous and normal. You have the power to join us in making it so.

This is what I believe. What is it that you believe? Belief is power. Belief will cause a person to take or avoid certain actions and endeavors. Anyone beginning an entrepreneurial effort of any variety is doing so for their own reasons that are unique to them and their dreams and while all of our interests, dreams and motives differ, what connects us is our belief that what we are working toward is not only possible to achieve but necessary for our life and will offer some special meaning. What other reasons would anyone do anything at all if they didn't first believe it to be achievable? There would never have been a Ford Motor Company if Henry Ford didn't first see the vision and believe in his heart that one day America would be driving around in what was then called motorized carriages. Because no matter if you think you can or if you think you can't, you're right. One could argue truer words have never been spoken.

Belief is power but belief is hard. Belief is tough. It's very tough to maintain because you're one day going to be confronted with questions posed to yourself about your own life. "Is this REALLY going to work"? "Am I wasting my time"? "What am I doing wrong"? "Why is this happening to me"? and "What can I do about it"? It is during these stressful times of massive doubt, when you're facing what seems to be insurmountable odds and its just problem after problem and even more things seem to come out of the woodwork, it is what you do in these moments that will determine your outcome and will affect the likely hood of success. Important to note that I'm writing this as someone who is on his way to and believes in yet has not physically seen the mountaintop. I am working to achieve the 1st ever Omaha Ambassador Trek, living each day working toward what I know to be inevitable. This is my dream and my effort to leave a legacy in my community. With your dreams you must perform each day with a level of certainty that increases over time no matter what setbacks you've had or times you've failed which will be more than you think. I believe it to be this generation that will reach into the historical record and find strength, motivation and tools to galvanize their compatriots and upon the authority of their own, do good for goodness sake.

Outlooks, Effort and Energy

When you want to be successful as bad as you want to breathe then you will be successful.

– Eric Thomas

The quest that is our lives is finite. It's ever changing, unpredictable and contains more twists, turns and unanticipated outcomes than can be expected. During this quest, what amount to goals for some and missions for others evolve as we all do, sporadically, suddenly, surprisingly and throughout this evolution we come to know and accept that no matter the planning, prayer or preparation that we undertake things that can and definitely will go awry more than a few times. There will be times when giving it all we've got wont be enough and we will fall short of our destinations but not our destiny. And it's the distinction and understanding of the two which will determine our individual and collective fortunes, much as the popular phrase indicates, sometimes stuff happens and it's in these moments when we're near knee deep in the stuff we discover more of ourselves and our world than at any other time. Only under enormous pressure and hostile conditions can what amounts to crude rock eventually become the beautiful diamond a man gives to the woman of his dreams. Only under pressure and hostile conditions served up by life will a man come to know if he can not only purchase that diamond, that piece of former raw earth, but to provide the life for her and himself that he envisions.

The pressure and hostile conditions that form these diamonds will likewise mold and mend us into what we inevitably become. Though we have little control of the events and circumstances that befall us we have absolute and total control over our responses to the pressure and hostile circumstances that happen to us every single day. What we each control most are our attitudes and how we go about the rigors of life in spite of not due to. If it is our attitude that determines our altitude, as suggested by a wise person once, then the choice to either sink or swim or to levitate and rise above the drama and succeed at all cost is ours alone. I've no intent to be cliché but we cannot control the hands that we're dealt. We can merely learn to play the cards we do have better and enhance our graciousness whatever the outcome, win or lose and if we do lose, to know that it's okay. Though we do not choose to lose we do choose to lose like winners. To lose like a winner actually means to recognize the ability to face the pressure yet not succumb to it, to fail yet feel the fear of trying and failing again and doing it anyway. Indeed, storms will come, dissipate and come again. How we ride out those storms that will become the measurement of our character and indication of our untapped resilience.

It's hard but worthwhile to practice these things. It goes beyond merely thinking positive or just being generally optimistic. It's about having your worst nightmare occur while living and maintaining Gods grace. Though we weather the storm we marvel at the miracle of our survival of it. Yea though we walk through the valley of the shadow of death we field the blessing of being able to walk, to walk right out of deaths valley and hike to the peaks of victory.

To get to where we want to go we've got to believe even when it's unbelievable. When things go wrong it's easy to be depressed. Its easier still to wallow in self-pity, walking around defeated and condemned thinking that the best life has to offer is a swift kick in the butt. Just because some things in our lives are negative doesn't mean that we should live our lives within the negative. You might be down on your luck and you may have been down for a long time but after a while you've got to realize that existing within the negative is too costly and taxing to your body and your spirit. At some point you've got to laugh at what used to make you cry. Sure you've got to deal with the challenges of the present but in this beautiful struggle you begin to do what good church folk always advise us to do, not let the devil steal our joy.

I believe Rocky Balboa says it best when speaking to his son in part 6 of the series after his son has a career setback. *"The world aint all sunshine and rainbows. It's a very mean and nasty place and it will beat you to your knees and keep you there permanently if you let it. Not me, you or nobody is gonna hit as hard as life. But it aint about how hard you hit, it's about how hard you can get hit and keep moving forward."*

Our time on earth much like the choices we make is precious, should not be wasted and are capable of both good and bad. Existing in the eye of the hurricane is neither desirable nor easy but within the epic calamity that can be our lives in moments of duress we reaffirm our capacity for stoicism and embrace the beautiful struggle that is life and dream pursuit. Success comes from failure. Surly no man succeeds at greatness without falling short enough times to make more proficient the talents and skills necessary to ascend to the highest levels of dream fulfillment. Practice never makes perfect. Practice only makes progress and as our long departed brother Mr. Frederick Douglass so once eloquently said, **"Without Struggle There Is No Progress!"**

Life's failures are people who did not realize how close they were to success when they gave up.

—Thomas Edison

CHAPTER 4

GROWTH

Most people engage in low life living. Low risk living. If you're not willing to risk, you cannot grow. If you cannot grow, you cannot become your best. And if you cannot become your best, you can't be happy. And if you can't be happy, then what else is there?

— **Les Brown**

GROWTH is about more than the physical. It is about our innate ability to consciously develop, progress and advance in our physical beings but our abilities extends to all aspects of life and more. We can grow in our intellect, our compassion, our ability to reason, in our humanity, spirituality and faith, in health, wellness and the whole of our personhood. The more you know the more you grow. You must be so knowledgeable about your craft, so enthusiastic and informed that you are considered an expert in your industry. You must pursue the information to ascend to this level and the pursuit of anything does not first happen without taking the first step. Mother Teresa once said "*Yesterday is gone. Tomorrow has not yet come. We have only today. Let us begin."* One cannot set eyes upon other shores without first boldly heading out to sea. We must be willing to do more than just step outside the box. The world is too big to remain in the same area not experiencing, not breathing, not seeing, not doing greater things among the wonders that make up our world. God didn't make the world for us to only see the same 2-10 miles each day to work or school. He didn't create Italy for the Italians. It's all for everyone. The only thing stopping you from getting there is you.

This book is as much about starting your own business and launching your own innovative ideas as it is about personal inspiration to encourage you to get off your butt and do something fulfilling for you. Economically speaking, we are living in historic times. Bleak news on the jobs front, slow economic growth and a host of challenges natural and man-made seem to overtake us constantly. There are many problems that our country must face head on if we are to survive and lead the global community in this new world that's being created each day. I want you to be motivated to do something extraordinary. I want you to be inspired to be bold in your dreams, daring in your efforts through massive action. I want you to be fulfilled in all of your personal aspirations and I very much want you to be prosperous and well in your financial futures. This is why I am a strong advocate of entrepreneurism and business ownership.

Most all businesses have employees and if you are to have your own business then it's very likely that you will one day need and hire employees. Employees are important. Employees are the backbone of all labor and the strong economy of the United States. This very crucial element of our economic society must never be undervalued, underappreciated or under estimated. My purpose is to inspire you to look at what and where you are and what you can become if you are diligent in your efforts and believe as all the greats of our past have done. I feel it to be wrong that our young people are pushed into a worldview and perspective that says all that they should look forward to is advancing the ideas, visions and plans of others; to "get a good job" and become another cog in the machine that is our society. The message that our school systems promotes, that our whole society promotes is to obtain enough education to further enhance the status quo and not to become the builders of the future and the leaders of the masses which is what I'm encouraging you to do. To do the opposite is to just follow conventional wisdom and in all of human history, all the greats have done the opposite of what conventional wisdom would have had them do. Your life is your life so please live it while you've got it.

I urge you to work diligently in making real your unique visions, dreams and businesses. Independent business ownership is a great and powerful thing and as I advocate your contribution to society through positive actions I'm also advocating the start up of the business venture you have inside you. We should work to make better the quality of human life but in our doing so there is nothing wrong with working to improve your lifestyle. It doesn't take much to change a person's lifestyle. If you increased the average persons monthly income by just a 1,000 dollars you will see some drastic improvements in that person's lifestyle. These improvements could be coming to your life if you develop and maintain the courage to push an idea into the future.

Learn all you can. We are affected by what we know. Don't be lazy in your learning. Don't be lazy in building your library, going to classes and gravitating to knowledge. When you're in school you should get the information while you're there. Nothing worse than being stupid when you get out of school. Being broke is bad but being stupid is what's really bad. Unless you're broke and stupid.

—*Jim Rohn*

It takes guts to step onto the world stage and ask people to not only trust you and your product or your service but to also buy it. That's what business is. You're asking someone to believe in you and your idea so much that they will pay to have what you offer. What scares many people is that no matter how great the idea, no matter how needed the service, no matter the depth of undiscovered value, people remain dominated by fear of rejection. We don't like being rejected. We don't like people telling us no. I'm telling you that if you are to be successful you must feel the fear and do it anyway. There will always be those who will be staunchly skeptical and will tell us no, but there are those who will see the vision and believe as we do and they will tell us yes! But you cannot get to the yeses if you do not first go through the no's. You might be reading this and thinking "this all sounds great but what if I believe, take these actions and nothing happened." I say, what if you believe, take massive positive action and something does happen?

Something I learned a long time ago during my many business experiments is that if you do something often enough, a ratio will appear. It's called the *Law of Averages* and if you do something consistent enough and if after each time that you attempt to make your sale or persuade another to adopt your idea and to invest into it, you continually refine your approach and re-configure your method you will get through the no's and find the yeses. I learned this lesson well as I began to market and sell copies of the first book that I was a part of, *Ready Set Succeed: Making Your Dream Come True*.

The law of averages, when combined with the passionate persistent perseverance of a dedicated mind will see you through. If you talk to 10 people you sell 1. You talk to 10 more people you get 1 more. Talk to 10 more people you get 2. Talk to 10 more people you get 3. Talk to 10 more people you get 5. What's happening here? Why would you get 5 the last time? You're getting better! Who among us has the power and ability to get better and improve their ratio? Anybody! Everybody! Anybody who puts in the effort. You will learn that the Law of Averages can be increased and that you can improve and enlarge your ratio of yeses to no's with positive massive action. Great success is born out of failure as you learn more through failure than you do by winning.

A business idea is a new life, like a newborn baby. Your vision, your mission; that is your new baby. If you love this baby as all parents should and most do, then you must take care of this baby. You must love and care for this baby as a father and mother would for their son. This new life, your business or social initiative must be nourished and protected as a mother and father would do such things. This creative new idea must be defended from the never-ending onslaught of encroaching voices who seek to talk you out of it.

Our unique ideas are born of a revolutionary ingenuity and are the bridges connecting the past with the future and linking the one generation to the next. You can never know how far your dream may travel and the impact if may have on the future long after our time in this place is done. Our ideas truly are the bridges allowing us to cross into the light and away from the darkness, toward the sun and away from the shadows.

The ability, power and harmonious ferocity of a good idea unleashed upon the world, backed by the blessed might of massive positive action is strength undefeatable. Though at times our plans and efforts may go awry, if there are necessary changes that have to be made the blessing is that those changes can begin today. Create and maintain a unique idea and/or product, talk about its merits, persuade someone it is a great deal and will add value to them and they then agree to buy, that's the simple act of sales. Sales is showing something you have or have discovered with others and doing it well enough to where they agree that they would like to participate. College students are taught that they need to learn how to sell themselves. This is of course referring to selling their unique talents and skills to prospective employers. A college graduate goes on to sell his/her skills to a prospective company for a wage or salary.

You have great skills that you are capable of bringing to bear and those skills combined with your ideas and massive action can be sharpened and help you to advance. Selling your idea, your imagination, your business, is possible. The proof of this is in everything around us as all things experienced at one point never existed until someone dreamed them up and made it so. It's possible that you can have more than you posses and become more than you are. The late great motivator and entrepreneur Jim Rohn once said of his success before passing *"I spent the first 6 years of my career working and I wound up broke. I make some changes and in the next 6 years I wound up rich. My first presentation was not that good. It was actually pretty lousy. It was so bad that if I were not the one doing it I would have gone home. But you know what, I did it again. I revised my method, and I did it again and I did it again and I did it again. That's the secret to how I got here."*

No matter the dream or vision that you yearn to see brought into the real, it can happen. It's possible!

A CROSSOVER STORY

Farrah Gray

The veil of impossibility must focus on what's possible and not what might go wrong. Sometimes we feel it is better to never try than to try and fail. These are complex emotions. But we must still confront our own self doubt and recognize that our destinies are in our hand. Real change happens when ordinary people get sick and tired of being sick and tired and finally DO SOMETHING!

— Michelle Obama

Some people are very self driven and self-motivated. They are naturally inquisitive and seek to do amazing things even from a very young age. While some need to be exposed to the curious wonders of our world and inspired by others to take action, others are truly natural-born business leaders. If you're reading this book I've got to believe that on some level that you're seeking something. You've got a dream or are dreaming of having a big dream to accomplish. No matter you're position in life, the trials, tribulations, efforts and energy, indeed the stories of others who have bled, fought and overcome what appeared to be unbeatable serve as inspiration to us all engaged in our own beautiful struggles. Discouragement comes when we approach an effort, try our hardest, and give it our all and still come up short somehow. We need the success stories of others to reinforce our own beliefs when we weaken. It helps to be able to say: If she can do it, I can too." I myself am working toward the greatest endeavor of my life; building a school in Malawi, East Africa. With Build On and their ambassador trek program I think often to myself, "If Oprah Winfrey can build a school, I can too." If Chris Rocks wife Maalack can build a school in Africa, SO CAN I"! It helps to be able to look at others succeeding in an area we are heading, see their success and know that in our own moments of strife and struggle that we are not crazy, that what we seek to accomplish can in fact be done. IT'S POSSIBLE!

Dr. Farrah Gray is an example of someone who upon his own initiative took his limited resources and began selling his own homemade brand of lotion at the age of 6! His biography is certainly impressive as he got in on the tech business early on through founding his own pre-paid phone cards, the one stop mail boxes services and more franchises as well as a youth oriented teen talk show on the radio. This is just the start of this mans life. He goes on to become the executive producer of a comedy show on the Las Vegas strip. Oh, and I can't leave out that he created his own youth oriented food company called Farr out Foods generating sales of over one million dollars.

His personal accolades are very impressive and while it would be marvelous for us all to begin companies generating millions and doing it before we are eligible to get a driver's license, as great as that would be it's not about the money or the material. It's about our own unique goals and desires, and our own concepts of new world wonders and realities. Whatever those things are, that is what you should relentlessly pursue to do. Certainly there has got to be something in your head that refuses to exist only there. Something in your mind yearns to breathe free in actual nature within our reality. The life and business of Dr. Farrah Gray should be a lesson to us all. That lesson should be never stop learning, earning and yearning! We must crank up our internal motors and refuse to quit! If this man achieved as much as he did as young as he was just imagine what you're capable of doing at this very moment. You must act because you could be living your dream lifestyle sooner than you think! What would you attempt to do if you knew you would not fail? Seriously answer this question. The success and dream fulfillment exercises at the end of the book will offer more.

Today Dr. Gray is a multi-millionaire and philanthropist gifting positive financial and inspirational examples in motion on a daily basis. He did what he wanted and needed to do. You must do what you know you must do to make your heart most happy!

Either you are going to believe in something, believe in a system or person or business and invest your time/money in it and go for it or you're going to believe in nothing, sit there and fall apart.

—Dell Gines

CHAPTER 5

RESPONSIBILITY

A lot has been given to you and a lot is expected out of you.

— *Joseph G. Smith, Sr.*

No matter if you know it or not, you were born with a debt. It's a sum larger, more meaningful and significant than any monetary amount. Its total is such that no matter what manner of work we engage in or complete through the duration of our lives, it can never be repaid. This **RESPONSIBILITY** is born of the lives sacrificed and blood spilled on behalf of us all throughout history. Surely heaven is filled with the souls of those who laid down their lives for we, their descendants to have the opportunities that we have and live the lives that we do. Understanding, accepting and living up to our social responsibilities brings honor to the glorious dead while simultaneously makes our world better thereby improving the quality of our lives. There will never come a time in which we can relax from our eternal responsibilities because the job, our social responsibilities are to make the world better in every way we're able, to do so through the power manifested in our interests and talents.

We need to use our power and help others understand that they have the ability to create and shape the world into the place that we believe it ought to be. We see the Mohandas Ghandi quote often "*be the change we want to see in the world.*" This is a great statement and is true indeed and the fastest way to change the world is to change ourselves. We need to know and understand that our descendants, those who have yet to be born will only have whatever we create for them. We have available to us what our ancestors and parents have created for us and it is our duty now to use whatever we do have to create a more peaceful world and shared prosperity for all and those who've yet to come.

We cannot afford to remain on the sidelines of history while others write it for us. Ascending to our proper placement in life is no easy task. To create the heavenly like conditions we seek is more than hard. Living life under circumstances not of our own choosing is even harder. We can at times become over wrought with second-guessing and doubt not knowing if our efforts are futile, constantly asking ourselves "will this ever work"? Only if we keep up the pursuit will it ever work. We have the power to usher into existence our dreams and bring about a new reality for ourselves, those we love and indeed the world. Once we begin to see our dreams realized piece by piece, the wonders of God become more real, personal and our faith will be increased and in our minds as what was once possible has now become inevitable. What you are working toward becomes certain to a degree not thought of before. Our faith, our certainty, our unwavering and belief in the possible impossibilities are the building blocks of our staircases to heaven. A staircase leading to the possible and productive futures we seek for ourselves and will ultimately remake our world for the betterment of all.

Get busy living or get busy dying. Strong and true words spoken by Tim Robbins character in the film *The Shawshank Redemption*. That statement is relevant to what we do with our time here on earth and weather or not we strive to make a genuine difference in the world. In my view we are either constantly engaged in the beautiful struggle for progress or allowing life to just happen as it is rather than shape it into what we know it must become. The later is dying the former is living. If you don't have a dream and are not working toward something larger than yourself or something you've never had, you're dead. Sure you are physically alive, you are breathing and taking up space and it can be called life technically, but is it really? What man is a man who does not make the world better? What life is a life not dedicated to personal and intellectual growth and fulfillment?

If at this moment the reasons for your life have yet to be revealed, if you feel incomplete, inadequate or otherwise unsatisfied because of some goal or desire continues to elude you, can you really remain on the sideline of history doing nothing and just accept the continual dissatisfaction? There is only one logical choice and that choice is to act. Choosing to act means dedicating yourself to making yourself and the place you dwell, better.

In our time and on this world Gods hands truly are our own and the manifestation of his goodness and the bestowing of his blessings will correspondingly come through us. Someone somewhere is in need of and awaiting a blessing that we have been charged to deliver. Blessing those around us by doing good, blesses us in turn. We've got to exercise our faith by helping others get what they need so that we may attain the things that we want.

What will it take to reach our young people? What is the catalyst that will spark change in the hearts and minds of the people who will one day grab hold the reigns of power in efforts to lead our country into a more fruitful future? These questions have many answers and there are many wonderful organizations and thoughtful people in those organizations who are dedicated to just that, helping our young people understand who they really are and what they are really capable of.

A component of achieving this goal is instilling the value of service within the minds of each child as early in their life as possible. Learning how to grow into a young man or a young woman who chooses to love and to uplift their fellow human being is the greatest ability and action that we can pass on to our youth. When you begin to serve others and to help others become what they wish, you also inherently serve yourself with the often not so intangible results of personal growth, enlightenment and a development of human capital that is beyond measure. It all starts with a vision. The Bible says: *Where there is no vision, the people perish*. **Proverbs 29:18.**

A vision I must share and communicate to you is that the stories you read and hear about on the nightly news and in the paper will be stories of the courageous triumph of our young people over the ills our society routinely serves up; that our youth will do more than survive but THRIVE! The service we offer others is the rent that we pay to occupy our place on the planet and for too long too many have paid more than their fair share of the rent required of all of us. We must push and push harder to open the doors of opportunity to all not simply those who were fortunate enough to be born to wealthy parents or born within the borders of a country that offers paths to prosperity. We must not forget the poor and in response to tough economic times balance our budgets on their backs.

Our generation is master of both the education and the whole body of circumstances of the generation coming after us. We cannot make them perfectly good and wise because we are in large measure deficient in goodness and wisdom so our efforts can at best be only to make them as good as or only slightly better than we are so as to continue the grand movement that is human evolution physically as well as with intellectual thought. We are in very real danger of allowing the next generation of people to inherit the Earth to fall below our own standard of living. In many countries life expectancies have begun to come down, more and more people are falling through the cracks, that is if they were ever seen at all. Truly the accurate measurement of our lives will be taken in what we did with our time here and how hard we've worked and what we've done for others beyond ourselves. For those of us who are striving for the top, we must remember to offer others a hand up.

A CROSSOVER STORY

Moses

The LORD shall fight for you, and ye shall hold your peace

— Exodus 14:14

Success is born out of failure, great struggle and what seems to be, in certain moments, insurmountable challenges. Sometimes we can be on a path to where we are sure we must go and through a series of unfortunate events or poor choices it appears that we have gotten so off track, made so many mistakes and had so many failures that we can never self correct enough to get back on the original path. In those moments that can last a long while in a person's life we must never give in to the doubt that fights to take hold or to the fear in our mind that aims to grow roots. We must overcome our shortcomings, setbacks and insecurities and shake off what we may have done wrong and focus in this moment on what we can get right. We cannot succeed burdened by guilt. Life is full of shoulda coulda wouldas. You can't go on condemning yourself for what you did or should have done. You might wish to have spent more time with your family, been a better spouse, wished that you had finished college or not passed up a good business deal due to fear or some other deep regret; either way you must let that go and be your best today!

Though our problems may be large our resources are plentiful. The mountain might be very high but it can be climbed. The real truth is that no matter the size of our dream we have what we need to overcome. Sometimes we begin looking for a way that appears to be far off when we should be looking closer to us. Most of us have heard the story of Moses. You may not know all the details but perhaps you've seen the Disney film The Prince of Egypt and remember the story of the gray bearded man leading the Israelites out of Egypt and when surrounded by mountains, the vastness of the red sea and pharaoh intent on massacre and in that moment, with the help of God, Moses used what was close to him, his staff, to overcome what only moments before appeared to be insurmountable.

Like Moses, we aim to achieve something amazing. Your dreams may not be to lead an entire people out of bondage but to you and for you, to achieve your goal, this great thing would be as significant. And that is good. It's good to have goals and designs that are grand in scope. No matter what mistakes we've made, there is nothing that can prevent us from overcoming what we face so that we can live out the purpose for which we were born. In his case, Moses spent 40 years on the backside of the desert. I'm sure he must have felt like a failure; wandering around, searching and not finding. The experience of Moses is an example of how our trials that we think are meant for our harm really are blessings in disguise meant to prepare us for the final stretch of the journey. Each one of us has our own unique burdens and hardships. The same as we all have unique voices and Unique fingerprints we also are so special that there can only be one of us. Even identical twins have features that are unique to themselves. The real truth of life is that we are the jewels of the earth. We may have gone through some hard times and some extreme difficulties and setbacks, but all that means is that we need a bit of polishing. We become polished people by not only correcting the mistakes of our past but also by adopting new disciplines for the future.

I love seafood but don't particularly care for clams. I'm a shrimp lover. While I love endless piles of shrimp I admire very much the clam. Clams feed on things at the bottom of the ocean and every once in a while clams will get a very tiny grain of sand in its mouth. Clams don't like the sand in their mouth. When a grain of sand does make its way in there the clam responds by trying to get rid of it. It is trying to expel what has become an irritant, the sand. It tries very hard. Sometimes it is successful and other times it is not so successful. It is only under the rough conditions of being poked, prodded and fought against with great pressure does that grain of seemingly meaningless sand reacts to the clams reaction by toughening up and becoming polished enough until that sand is no longer sand but instead a beautiful pearl. That is what you are, a beautiful pearl!

People pay a lot of money for pearls, ladies like to wear them around their necks and while material possessions are not most important, pearls have become status symbols in and of themselves. But those beautiful pearls would never have become what we know as valuable had they not undergone the constant poking, prodding and outside agitation that was only temporary. That which we struggle against and battle with will oppose us only temporarily and not forever.

I'm suggesting that you reevaluate your life and think differently about the problems and challenges you must overcome and adopt a new view that can help you not only succeed but to do it faster than if you keep and maintain a pessimistic, negative and defeatist mindset. Sometimes we must weather the storm but other times we need only recognize that we already may have at our disposal what's needed if we could only see it. Could it be that you already have what you need to overcome? God wanted Moses to lead the people of Israel out of bondage and he thought he didn't have what it took to achieve such a thing. He didn't think he had what he needed, that Pharaoh and the people of Israel themselves would not listen and that someone else was better suited for the job. He believed that he had made too many mistakes and that with as much time as he had spent on the back side of the dessert in exile that his time for any sort of relevance had passed and that he had gotten too old (he was 80 years old at the time of the Exodus) to fulfills God's promise and that while he had once believed he was meant for a great purpose that he has now somehow missed his chance. We now know this wasn't the case, as in every instance God provided all that he needed, the staff that he already had.

Could it be that right now the greatest obstacle you face is your own fear and lack of action? No matter how devastatingly daunting our circumstances may seem, we have at our disposal right now the combined might of our creativity, ingenuity and bravery that can outthink, outwit and out match any problem! For sure no weapon formed against us shall prosper when pitted against a determined human mind…your mind! You have the power to achieve what you believe. It's possible!

Until the great mass of the people shall be filled with the sense of responsibility for each other's welfare, social justice can never be attained

— Hellen Keller

CHAPTER 6

ENERGY

It shouldn't take someone 30 years and an ultimatum from their doctor to realize that exercise is important. That we, the human body, was made to move so that we might live and last and love longer.

— Joseph Glenn Smith, II

I'm fast approaching my 6-year fitness anniversary since I began my exercise program and worked to change my health for the better and I'm very pleased with my results thus far. I still have a long way to go to reach my goals but at one point I honestly never really thought I would get here. Here being to the point in which I can actually see my abdominal muscles. I don't even know how many times I've said it, "I just want to get a 6 pack."

There are before pics, after pics and there are in-between pics and the recent photos I've added to my facebook page are my in between pics. A photographic progress report. I needed to add some new pictures anyway but I was looking in the mirror and couldn't believe what I looked like. I was amazed because I know what I looked like before. All the exercise in and out of the gym that I have put in over the years has worked. It is working now! This is important for several reasons, mostly because it proves that *Passionate Persistence Pays Plenty.*

I've tried a variety of supplements, different exercises and talked with numerous personal trainers and fitness enthusiasts who were/are vastly ahead of me and through it all; through every setback, the ebbs and flows of weight fluctuation and especially the seemingly endless moments of sheer frustration of being stagnant, of running in place not losing any weight, what has been the most effective element of my success is that I never gave up! I've kept going, kept searching, kept thinking about the solution to the setbacks I faced that were blocking me from getting to where I was trying to go. Yet in spite of all my frustrations, time and time again I just kept at it. It really is true that *Passionate Persistence Pays Plenty.*

Success in the area of physical fitness means and is different for each different person, and to achieve success you must know that different strategies will work for some but not for others. Each of us must decide what formula we will use to achieve our desired results. Not giving up and consistently moving forward has been and is the real key ingredient to reaching the current level I now reside and has given me the most meaningful results thus far. Only after beginning such a challenge with a new outlook and determination to overcome what I had surrendered to all my life is this possible. Of all the proteins, fat burners and an assortment of other pills, powders and products all promising to help you look your very best butt naked, in the end it's YOU who must put in the work.

I've written all of this because I am proud of my achievements. While I'm not yet where I want to be (10% body fat), I and all of my friends who are struggling with their weight or weight loss regimen need and/or lack encouragement. I'm saying to you that *Passionate Persistence Pays Plenty.* I'm encouraging you to stay in faith and rededicate yourself to yourself over and over and over; again and again and again if need be because success is possible. Success is possible But success is P.R.O.G.R.E.S.S. and progress takes patience. Progress take time. Progress takes prayer. Progress takes sacrifice. But Progress comes! We each are creating and living our own personal story of victory or defeat based on the choices we make. Choose today to become the leaner, cleaner, healthier, wealthy and passionate you that you've always wanted to become. I made the right choice and so can you!

There must be a physical fitness component to our dream fulfillment plans. It's important to maintain a balance and equilibrium to our life. Health and wellness applies to our physical bodies as it does to our mental and emotional selves. Each year many people go through the same ordeal as the New Year approaches and they start to make resolutions about changing all the bad habits or vigorous adoption of new habits that have long been talked about but never amounted to anything beyond mythology. The promises of exercising and eating healthy and quitting smoking and spending more time at home are all made and all too often fall by the wayside as the pressing demands of life continue to dog us while we're unable to keep up and properly prioritize. The reality is that you need not wait for a new year to make a life change, to do the things you've long knew you should have been doing or wanted to do. Today can be the first day of that new year. The most committed certainly wins so too does the early bird get the worm. When it comes to your dreams you must get started now!

Living out the opening days and hours of our personal new year we leave behind all that's transpired in the previous one; our achievements, our goals left unmet and resolutions that have fallen by the wayside. We forge new thoughts and dreams for this new chapter in the evolving books that are our lives. While the themes of our thoughts are commonly shared by many, the start of a new year means different things to each of us. For most it is a chance to start over, to untangle ourselves from our mistakes and poor choices of yester year and start anew. For others it is a chance to start doing the things we know we should have done or being the person we long should have been. No matter who you are the new year is certainly a time to let go of the baggage we've been carrying and begin anew, to believe again, to assert our abilities in the most productive manner possible; forging a better future for ourselves while inevitably illuminating the darkness offering sight to the next generation and to the blind of our own.

We live now at the start of the new decade with a blessed opportunity to make it as great as the last decade was bad. This decade must be claimed by each of us individually and collectively as a nation. The first ten years of this New Millennium have been beyond challenging for our country. Indeed for far too many this previous decade has been downright deadly as we saw the wicked success of evil with the attacks on 9/11. We witnessed the start of two wars, one waged in response to attack and in remembrance of lives lost and yet another which divided our nation over circumstances that are hotly contested to this day. The Great Recession of 2008 destroyed more than the retirement plans of our citizens but also ate away at the historical confidence of America that's been in place since the conception of the United States. That confidence, that overriding optimism, the intangible faith we have as Americans that we can do, suffer through and overcome whatever we must to get to where we want to be, to where we know we were born to be is what carried us through those troubled times and is what will propel us further into our glorious futures.

Our American identity and history is a testimony to all that we're capable of. We can and will bear any burden for our faith, families and freedom. Trek thousands of miles through the uncharted frontier in the dead of winter; no problem, willfully put your life on the line for the cause of liberty and freedom; sure thing, face down calls for your assassination and proceed with what you know must be done and actually do for the cause if it's a worthy one; you bet. That's just who we are as a people. That's the spirit of this great country in action. That's what it means to be an American.

Power cedes nothing without being demanded to do so and to get the change that we want, to take our lives into a different direction and have ownership over our destinies we must demand a greater performance level from ourselves. We have to begin to do all the things we know we should have done last year but didn't. Yes, it is time to claim ownership over our lives and fortunes and destinies by being new people in this new decade, but we've got to do something that's new to many of us and that is to stick with it. We've got to have stick-to-itiveness. It's not enough to start. It's not even enough to finish. We've got to start, get going and keep going and going and going further still. We've got to have the longevity to outlast the energizer bunny. Indeed we've got to become our own energizer bunnies with our own internal power sources dedicated to fueling our fortunate futures.

Each new day presents new opportunities as well as new challenges as each new year and new decade offer the opportunity to prove and present to the world new truths. These truths center around one major truth which is that we all, every single one of us, are endowed with an inner ability, a power to change our lives, change the world and depending upon the technology that someone younger will create, change the universe.

Over the course of our shared history one theme has been prevalent more than any other and that is that everything ever thought impossible by humans has been turned on its face by others through the stubborn and passionate persistence of those who knew better, who knew it could be done, who looked at what's been called impossible and saw was instead inevitable. Think the Earth is the center of the universe? Don't tell that to Galileo. For those who believed self-propelled machines would never replace the power and carrying capacity of horse and buggy systems, Henry Ford had some words for them. Didn't think America would ever have a Black president? Martin Luther King, Jr. did and predicted we'd have one in 40 years during an interview with the BBC in 1964. You can see and hear his prophetic words by searching www.YouTube.com for MARTIN LUTHER KING PREDICTED A BLACK PRESIDENT BBC REPORT.

When our current thought processes and actions, efforts and strategies, plans and projects no longer yield the results we need or are aiming for, it is time for the development and adoptions of new systems and ideologies for the better advancement and safeguarding of our desired futures. We cannot begin this new start in this new decade with old actions and even older thoughts and life perspectives. This will not suffice for bringing about the new realities we seek.

If in this new start your desire is to be a new you, you've got to develop, adopt and sustain a new view. As we do this individually, we must do this collectively as a nation seeking to hold onto and expand upon its greatness. It is not enough to merely tell others and chant amongst ourselves that we are #1. We must go through the beyond difficult process of actually becoming #1 and you do this through rigorous study, exercise, debate, research, development, prayer and consistency.

The way in which I fell into exercise as a hobby was not by accident but not on purpose either. I started working out with my friend and after some weeks of doing it I started noticing small changes. After a few months I started noticing some big changes. I liked very much all the changes. I started working out because I wanted to look better. I wanted more **ENERGY**. That was my motivation then and it is my motivation now. Don't get me wrong, I want and need to be healthy and I'm glad that I am, but for me looks are my main motivator. Perhaps that's kind of vain but my reasons for exercise are unique to me as yours should be unique to you. What's important is that you do have a reason. You must have a reason for doing something. My message to you is to find your reasons and get started. Get past all the things that have and are preventing you from getting moving and achieving something special and meaningful in your life, in and out of the gym.

You were not born to live life existing under the crushing weight of disease, stiff and sore joints and a lack of ability to perform at desired levels. You know we have a problem in America when over 25 million children have diabetes. The center for Disease control estimates that by the year 2050 1/3 of all Americans will have diabetes. That's unacceptable! Diabetes means a shortened life span, diabetes means suffering a preventable hardship and unnecessary medical costs.

I don't need to beat you down with negative statistics for you to understand that your body needs and benefits from regular and vigorous physical movement. Long before what we now refer to as a civilization human beings used to hunt for their food. There was no burger king drive up window. People hunted and fished every single day because there was no pizza delivery…ever. The physical exertion of working to maintain your life was all someone needed and while the human species has evolved and adapted over the years we still have the same functions and the same needs. We are now as we were then compiled of 70% water and we still need to have the regular exertion of physical exercise to be healthy and ward off disease. You've got to make the important decision to eat healthy and live healthy. How you do it and what diet and exercise regimen you follow will be decided as you go along. Those things are not the important factor anyway as what remains paramount is that you take action. Realize that you can look better, feel better, live better and just be better if you make that decision and take MASSIVE ACTION in all areas in business, in education and in fitness. Besides, when you start working out you'll soon find that you actually like it and that it was the best decision you ever made.

A CROSSOVER STORY

Wilma Rudolph

Nothing happens until something moves

— Albert Einstein

When we think of our dreams, what we must know above all is that our dreams and our goals, the important invisible things that appear so real to us in our minds; all those beautiful things can in fact happen. It's possible! Your dreams can actually, for real, come true. It's possible! The majestic symphony you've thought of orchestrating, It's Possible! The upscale restaurant you dreamt of opening, It's Possible! The weight that you want to lose, It's Possible! The traveling you've always wanted to do, It's possible! The submarine you want to command in the United States Navy, It's Possible! Becoming the fastest woman in the world, It's Possible!

We know these things are possible because others have done those very things. We know our dreams are possible because all great things were at one time nonexistent until someone dreamt them up and went about the business of making them come alive and exist in the real! Someone thought of something they believed in and made the Great Crossover of dream fulfillment. That story is told many times over in the lives of many extraordinary people as in a special story of triumph in the life of Wilma Rudolph, the first American woman to ever win 3 Olympic gold medals. Winning a gold medal is very special and noteworthy, let alone winning 3 of them and on top of that being the first to do it, but that's not the most inspiring part of her story.

Wilma Rudolph was an over comer. Born prematurely at only 4.5 pounds in 1940 to very poor and hardworking people, she was often very sick as a child being treated for measles, mumps, scarlet fever, double pneumonia and even polio! All of these illnesses are terrible in their own right and are life threatening but polio in particular was a scourge of eras gone by and eventually wiped out largely by an expansive vaccination program around the world. Her parents did the best they could to nurse her back to health as the local hospital at the time was for whites only and would not treat Wilma because she was black.

Her mother brought her to the doctor when it was discovered that her left leg was deformed and becoming weak she learned of her having polio, an illness with no known cure. The doctors told her family that she would never walk. With dreadfully horrific news ringing throughout her mind, Mrs. Rudolph, Wilma's mother, would not give up. She pursued treatment at Meharry hospital, the black medical college of Fisk University in Nashville, Tennessee. This facility was over 50 miles away yet they made the trek twice a week for two years until she was miraculously able to walk with the aid of a leg brace. During physical therapy and exercise at home with the blessed support of her brothers and sisters she became encouraged to be stronger and work harder and longer and through the power of constant, consistent MASSIVE ACTION she would walk normally by age 12. It was then she decided to become an athlete.

Wilma Rudolph went on to become a basketball star in high school leading her team to a state championship. Later she became a track star going all the way to attending her first Olympic games in 1956 at the age of 16! She won the bronze medal in the 4 x 4 relay, and on September 7, 1960, she became the first American woman to win 3 gold medals in the history of the Olympics!

Her story is one of achieving greatness in spite of. Her story is one of histories jewels shining through time offering a most wise light illuminating our own paths to our own tales of greatness in spite of. Certainly if Wilma Rudolph can overcome polio and a history of disease to become a great Olympic figure forever remembered, than you too can overcome what you must to achieve your happiness, to make real and have that which makes your heart most happy.

Just because something looks impossible does not mean that it is impossible. Just because someone says that it cannot be done does not mean it cannot be done. It only means that they have chosen not to do it but you have the power to make your own choices, follow your path and make history your own way. What would you attempt to achieve if you knew that you would not fail? The world is open to you. That which you have always seen with your minds eye and brought a smile to your face can be made real to be witnessed by your physical eyes. If you believe, if you take persistent, passionate MASSIVE ACTION, it will happen. IT'S POSSIBLE!

The higher your energy level, the more efficient your body, the more efficient your body, the better you feel and the more you will use your talent to produce outstanding results.

—Tony Robbins

CHAPTER 7

SUPPORT

The probability that we may fail in the struggle ought not to deter us from the support of a cause we believe to be just.

— Abraham Lincoln

Our best days lie before us. To bring these glory days to fruition, we need to be open to change, be willing to adapt to the varying circumstances of life while viewing our challenges through new eyes. Our country and we, each have ability to both destroy one another and save one another. There are those who see and approach global challenges believing that the only effective solutions will come through conflict; that only through the terrible rhythm of war can we once again know peace. I've a different view based upon a not so hidden truth that no matter its origins war produces victims, whom cling to hatred, who commit terrorism, which produces victims, whom cling to hatred and wage war, which produces victims, whom cling to hatred, who commit terrorism, which produces victims, whom cling to hatred and wage war. All of this serves the negative aim of our mutually assured destruction. Now is our time to make and live the change we want to see in the world and we must begin this task immediately.

While the opportunity to carry over the baggage from last year and the last decade exists so to does our chance to right the wrongs of yester year and usher in a new and blessed era of peaceful co-existence. I've got this new view and I pray that my countrymen, my brothers and sisters in Christ and fellow citizens of the world do too. All the conditions on Earth are the cumulative result of our collective action and inaction. Everything we do impacts and shapes the world in profound ways that in many respects are beyond our comprehension. A simple kind word of support can be the encouraging blessing that someone needs to make it through the trials they are going through. We must make a commitment to being the best and most respectful selves we can be. As a Christian I believe in both heaven and hell. I hope, pray and work so that when my time comes I will live out eternity with my lord and savior Jesus Christ. As a human being and citizen of the global community I'm well aware that the conditions we create, live, struggle and excel under, no matter if you are a Christian, Muslim, Buddhist or atheist, the choices that we make can create both heavenly and hellish conditions for us all. In the here and now the decisions we make are shaping what will be our grandchildren's future. In all of our daily actions we've got to think about the future and our descendents who've yet to arrive. When they look back and ponder upon what we their ancestors have done, will they be thankful and benefit from our work and exerted energies and appreciate our struggle to propel them forward or will they be cleaning up the mess we left behind and fighting our unfinished battles? What we do today will answer that question.

It's a sad affair when the most anyone thinks of their fellow human beings is during terrible natural disasters that are for moments saturated with news reporters only to be swept from the headlines once the next reality show star goes to court. Then as the holiday season comes upon us we are suddenly more compassionate than at other times. Thinking of and caring for each other is a great human trait that we should indulge in always not just the "Holiday Season." Thanksgiving is about more than the sales the morning after.

Thanksgiving encompasses many treasured values that we share as a country and culture symbolized best perhaps by the turkey, who for all pertinent purposes we'll call Tom. Now Tom, coming from the butterball clan, is a featured dinner guest within the homes of tens of millions of Americans, albeit as the main course. In spite of Tom being based and battered with all the fixings our grocery stores have to offer, there exists a harmonious relationship between that which will be devoured and we the devourers. It is during our familial gathering around Tom this time each year that we give thanks and celebrate one another and all the blessings we have but often go unappreciated and taken for granted. Through the year we lose touch during times of difficulty and stress with the people and events that do more than shape us but also give our lives special meaning and significance. It is around the dinner table, especially during this time of thanksgiving that families are reconnected, bonds are strengthened and if only for a moment we cast off the social restraints that keep us apart.

We know Thanksgiving by its many characteristics: The falling brown leaves, turkeys in abundance, and of course the countless sales commercials and deep discounted offers on everything from toys to the latest electronic widget that are all indicative of the holiday being upon us. Probably the most important indicator of all is not the turkey, but the Salvation Army bell ringers. They are the men and women who don winter gear and brave the cold night and day and day and night wielding Christmas bells as a nonverbal suggestion to give.

Giving. When you get past our flurry of travel and dinner plans, giving lies at that heart of our great American traditions. We give thanks for our blessings, we give money to the bell ringers and many others give their time volunteering for worthy causes. No matter if a person gives spare change to a bell ringer or construction materials to the habitat for humanity or give canned goods to a food drive we do so for over arching reasons because we want, we need, to bless others and improve the quality of others' lives as much as we can for as long as we can. Though hearts are more inclined to give during the holiday season we know that not only is giving the right thing to do, but also as we become a blessing in the lives of others we correspondingly bless ourselves. We know that in this life while our personal interests are always in front of us screaming for attention so too is our desire to be a credit to mankind during our time. Man cannot live on bread alone and we cannot live our life alone. Life is not about "me" it's about "we."

I give my thanks each day not just on Thanksgiving for all the blessings bestowed to me that have contributed to my being who I am, but for my family, friends, supporters and believers in me for all of my ideas and efforts, I give thanks and offer my prayers of Gods blessings for them in return. But I also must recognize, give credence to and express thanks for all our collective blessings that go unmarked but are of equal import. During this special time not long ago in 2010, the world stood shocked and stood upon a nervous edge in the aftermath of North Korean artillery strikes on civilians in South Korea bringing to a boiling point emotions and historical grievances that make possible the reigniting of war on the Korean peninsula. And while the desire for retaliation raged and the unwitting war-mongers were clamoring for conflict on television, I for one was thankful that for the moment at least, cooler heads had prevailed and all out war was averted. Certainly there are better methods of solving problems than destroying one another.

There are always going to be arguments and disagreements that boil over and bring us to the brink, but the development of young minds that will grow and become the cooler heads these volatile scenarios demand for a peaceful resolution, require constant nurturing and opportunities to be made aware of the people and the broader issues of the world at large. Our youth need opportunities to understand the importance of diplomacy and come to know that they can become the diplomats; that they can diffuse our global powder keg of possible conflicts and usher into existence what all people from all lands from all times have wanted … peace. I'm talking about the type of peace that makes life worth living. We are all Gods children. We all breathe the same air. We all cherish our children's future. We are all mortal.

So it is now as Christmas looms ever near and is followed by the celebratory start of a new year that we, The Omaha Dream Team, individually and collectively give thanks for all we have and our ability to exert our energies, talents and resources toward the betterment of others. We are thankful for the support we've been given and more thankful for the support yet to come and readily look forward to giving thanks next year for having the chance to build a school in Malawi that at the time of this writing is yet just a vision, a vision we are certain will create a glorious new reality.

I'm convinced that our world can be a more loving and equitable place. That the circumstances a person is born with or born into must not remain their burden to bear for the remainder of that person's life. Indeed positive changes can be made if each person is courageous enough to act upon what already is their human obligation to advance our race; the human race. I for one will do all I can and exert all of my energy to the cause of global life improvement, as the blessings bestowed to me are only the result of the hard work and many sacrifices of generations past.

I seek to enact the greatest amount of good for the greatest number of people as is possible for me to do. My work, my passions and even my life are only available to me because of the tremendous sacrifice made by others on my behalf. This Omaha Ambassador Trek is as much about our personal responsibilities to make life on Earth better as it is about the true demonstration of our own individual power and ability to achieve greatness on levels we've never thought possible.

A CROSSOVER STORY

John H. Johnson

*If it could happen to a Black boy from Arkansas,
it can happen to anyone.*

— John H. Johnson

What I like about history is that even though it's gone it's always with us. We take the past with us. The past lives within us — the good, the bad, the positive, the negative. What we do with the intergenerational aspects of history that we carry with us makes all the difference in our lives. We should not be burdened, defeated and condemned by the past but we can be if we choose to. We cannot change what's been done but we can forgive ourselves and others, and focus on being our best today. The history that shines most bright within our mind and stirs the soul like none other are the radiant examples of humanity and we human beings rising to the occasion accomplishing that which we all have within us and are capable of achieving. The history of us as in "we the people" provides the proof and the guiding inspiration that we need to give us power to fuel our fortunes and allow us to fly to higher heights. John H. Johnson stands in time with us today as such proof.

There is opportunity all around us, and it is for each of us to decide what we will do when opportunity presents itself. Opportunity comes often through the blessed support of others giving someone a chance. I'm not the only one who would love to get a "big break" but if you or I are to ever get that big break someone else most likely will offer it to you and you would then enthusiastically excel in that area and that moment would become the time in which you had your big break.

Born in 1918, the grandson of American slaves in rural Arkansas, John H. Johnson attended an overcrowded segregated elementary school. The highest level of education he could obtain was the eighth grade as there was no public high school for black people in his community. When it came time to end his schooling in the eighth grade he chose to repeat the eighth grade determined to learn more than he did the first time rather than go off to work in the same saw mill that killed his father when he was only 6 years old. He recognized the opportunity that education presented and seized it with righteous vigor. Looking for greater opportunities than what was available John moved to Chicago, Illinois with his mother and stepfather. As he attended a segregated high school his parents couldn't find any work. They struggled to support themselves for a long while, as those were very hard times. At school he was made fun of because of his country style of talk and dress. While enduring the pressure of becoming a young adult he discovered chances to learn about things other than labor at the sawmill. His high school career was distinguished by his leadership skills as he became student council president, editor of the school newspaper and class yearbook. He attended high school during the day and studied self-improvement books at night. Because of all he had achieved John H. Johnson was invited to speak to a dinner by the Urban League.

It was at the dinner and after hearing the Young man speak that the president of Supreme Life Insurance Company heard Johnson's speech and was so impressed that he offered him a job to help him through college. Starting out as an office assistant at supreme life he diligently worked to increase his presence and gained increasing responsibilities as time moved on. Among his duties was to prepare a monthly digest of newspaper articles for the company president Mr. Harry Pace. Doing this forced him to wonder if other people might enjoy receiving the information that Mr. Pace did. His inquisitive nature was nurtured as he was able to see first hand the day-to-day operations of a Black owned business which helped to foster his own dream of starting a business some day.

Like all dreams anyone may have the idea of ownership took hold within his mind and had begun to grow and he became determined only to go forward. His vision of his business and more importantly of his life as a business owner began to grow and enlarge further each and every single day. A young Mr. Johnson refused to be discouraged or lose faith in himself and his ideas even though he often was on the receiving end of negative forecasts from his peers. He always believed, he never gave up the vision; he never stopped planning, never stopped praying and never stopped paying his dues of extremely hard work, perseverance and dedication. When the time came to take an even larger step forward, he couldn't do it alone. He needed help. He needed help even though no one believed his ideas could take shape, would work or make any money. Only his mother, with a deeply biblical faith in God and in her son supported him. She allowed her son to use her furniture as collateral for a $500.00

loan. He used that loan to publish the first edition of Negro Digest in 1942.

Johnson did excellent in creating a smart, attractive and very much needed social product however he needed more **SUPPORT**. He had difficulty with distribution. Negro Digest needed to be circulated. That's when he met and partnered with Mr. Joseph Levey, a magazine distributor who was impressed by Johnson. With valuable tips and insights to greater exposure from Mr. Levey, Johnson was able to get his magazine on the news stands in other urban communities and within 6 months he reached a circulation of over 50,000!

Negro digest covered areas of social life and topics such as black history, literature, arts and culture. After years of publication the title was then changed from Negro Digest to Black World. This new publication achieved success in its own right with a circulation greater than 100,000 however; it was dwarfed by the mega success of what we now know as Ebony Magazine!

Being the hard working and creative man that he was he enjoyed his well-earned success while seeking further knowledge and becoming further inspired and taking greater massive action. With Ebony magazine doing exceptionally well it only made sense to create another product that would become a staple in the house holds of millions of Americans. He did this by creating Jet Magazine! As extraordinary as this is, Johnson wasn't done yet. He went on to become the CEO of Supreme Life Insurance Company. He purchased 3 radio stations, started a book publishing company, produced more magazines and even developed his own line of cosmetics. In it's 40th anniversary issue Ebony magazine had a circulation of over 2,300,000 and was a major contributing reason to Johnson becoming one of Forbes richest individuals in the United States.

What he did was truly remarkable and throughout this incredible story there are three very important things that made this possible. The 1st thing is that he had an unyielding desire to learn. Think about it, when nearly forced out of school he repeated the 8th grade rather than work at a sawmill. He sought extra help, he did extra work and he took greater initiative. Never in his life did this man ever stop wanting to know more. There is a lesson to be learned here.

The 2nd key element is that someone gave this man the opportunity to first be an office assistant. Mr. Pace who saw what he had done at the Urban League dinner all those years ago. Without that offer he never would have assembled that collection of articles and news content on Back American life that were the early beginnings of Ebony magazine and all his other ventures. Just think if he had never had this opportunity and Ebony magazine never was created. How would that impact not only his life but also our whole culture? It's important to remember that while we each are climbing the ladder of success to be sure to give someone else a hand up if you're fortunate enough to get to the top before they do.

Finally, the most critical element in making this all occur was Mr. Johnson's relentless application of all that he had learned. He just kept trying. He had very bold visions and with the blessed help of his mother he took the risk, stepped out on faith and went about the glorious business of making his dream come true. He saw and was offered opportunities and made the most of those opportunities. During an interview once he said about achieving success that you must "*convince people that it is in their best interest to help you.*" We all need help at times and if your dreams are as big and bold as they should be you're going to need help. The difference between mega success and never getting anywhere could be how hard and smart you are at finding the right support and being dedicated and faithful enough to your own visions to take massive action.

Opportunity is available to us all. We each do different things when presented with an opportunity but opportunities do come and opportunities do go. If we all start out in life in a sailboat, the factor that really matters in determining our destination is not the wind blowing at us but the set of our sail. The same winds blow on us all. The winds of change, the winds of disasters, the winds of opportunity blow on us all. You have the power to do the most amazing things no matter what happens and no matter the obstacle so long as you're willing to correct the mistakes of the past while adopting new disciplines for the future. As John H. Johnson once said *"if it could happen to a young black boy from Arkansas, it can happen to anybody."* It's Possible!

CHAPTER 8

SPIRITUALITY

One thing that I found out about human beings is that we don't know what we're truly made of UNTIL we're backed into a corner. UNTIL we're up against insurmountable odds. UNTIL we're as low as we could possibly be. That word until is a transitional word. See, you didn't know how strong you were UNTIL…you didn't know that you could in fact handle it UNTIL…you didn't know you could accomplish that UNTIL!!! That word UNTIL transitions us out and into something else.

— Quentin Whitehead Sr.

Faith is taking the first step even though you cannot see the staircase. Dr. Martin Luther king Jr. was correct in this statement and we all would be very well served in our attempts to live the meaning of these words. Attempting to do something that's never been done before is beyond difficult for many reasons chief of which are the never ending boisterous rants of others who insist to you that what you're working toward is impossible or that at best maybe meager steps forward can only be achieved and not total victory. But we must hold firm to our plans and goals no matter what as we seek to do what has never been done before all while tuning those voices out. Focusing on our love of God and forever clutching to our beliefs will see us through to our victory. Our faith is what will prove to the masses that what we aim to achieve is not impossible but inevitable. Young folk from our great city will travel to Malawi, East Africa and build a school in the first Omaha Ambassador Trek and this is inevitable!

There is much our Omaha Dream Team needs in terms of support. I don't have all the answers. All I've got is an unwavering love of God and faith that the people I need to partner with, the businesses whose advertising and sponsorship I'm seeking will cross my path at the appropriate time. Goal attainment does not occur by having faith and sitting on the couch waiting for Gods manifestation to appear and endow us with what we need. We have to work to exercise our faith. Faith without works is dead. Martin Luther King Jr. was one of the fiercest advocates for the poor in all of American history. For those who choose to study and know history, you will learn that he worked his faith through more than speeches and marches. For us in our time we have to be the fiercest advocate there is for the cause we choose to take up. We must fight for what we want because no one else will. No one will believe in you until you believe in yourself.

The last piece of my *PROGRESS PRINCIPLE* is **SPIRITUALITY**. I cannot encourage you to follow any particular doctrine of faith nor would I want to. Some of the greatest friends I've known are Muslims, Christians, Buddhists, agnostics and atheists alike. I write spirituality because as you make your way through life and work to get things done and achieve your dreams you will undoubtedly be hit with unforeseen circumstances and events. There will be hard times you must go through and overcome, barriers that seem to erect themselves overnight. These barriers, perhaps the one you're up against now will appear to be unbreakable, unshakable and when you call out for help from those who you believe in your heart will be there for you, you will find when life is at its most difficult that your calls will not be answered. Your voicemails will not be heeded or returned. All answers to your pleas will be "NO" and in these moments we will ask, what do I do now? Only in times of immense adversity do we ever truly appreciate and take notice of the small things we once took for granted.

The stranger who gives you a ride when you were walking in the intense heat and humidity, the church that opens its food pantry doors to you, the friend who gives you his slightly used shoes to replace the ones you were wearing that were completely worn out and ravaged from overuse, the friend who opens his doors to you when no one else will so that you may not go without shelter — all these things and many more are the great blessings from God that should not go unnoticed or unappreciated. At times in our lives, we may come to feel that the walls are closing in on us and that all of planet Earth has rejected us. This is in fact not true. The greatest resource we have is internal fortitude and our ability to be the blessing in the lives of others who are praying for someone to deliver them.

Our spirituality is important because we do not possess all knowledge. It is important because we do get weak, we do get tired and fatigued and disoriented, and for many people even suicidal; not because they are crazy but because they feel as if they have come to the end of their rope, that there really is nothing else they can do except to end it. These are but some of the reasons to believe in God, a higher power, a supreme being or just a secular connection to all that is within the universe. While we may be surrounded by people at times, but still feel utterly alone. You must have something to rely on to maintain and replenish your strength so as to be able to keep going to make it to yet another day that could very well bring about your victory that you have forever seen in your mind's eye.

I believe in God. But this is my life and my belief. But this is my life and my belief. You must live your life and come to know what are your own beliefs and what you will look to for gaining a deeper measuring of your own life and purpose. If you are reading this book it is because you are after something, you must have a vision of a creation stemming from your own mind that you yearn to see come into existence. This book is just that for me. The very fact of your holding this book in your hands, reading my words and looking at my picture, is a testament to the power of persistence and a loving God who is always with us and seeks to save and uplift us.

Remember that song, (I'm unsure of the name) but it goes "Nobody knows the trouble I've seen, nobody knows my sorrows"? This song has elements of truth in it for me as I am engaged in the single greatest battle of my life, the fight for the continuation of it! No person on earth in fact knows my struggle or the trouble I've seen but I know that God has. If he hadn't then you would not have this book in your hands now.

This chapter, this final plank in the *PROGRESS PRINCIPLE*, is about you discovering and knowing unto yourself that there is something bold and beyond yourself that you should reach out and tap into. You must discover what you will believe in and adhere to on your own terms but what I can say is that for me and my house, we will serve the Lord.

Faith, religion or spirituality is important in the context of what happens to and with our immortal soul as well as our intangible dreams. In relation to dream fulfillment and goal attainment, you will find that faith or meditation or even focusing on our being one with the universe is important because it can serve as a spiritual refueling for us when we are down and halfway out. These things serve as more than a stress reliever when we are at our boiling points they keep our internal motors running. Even if you suffer from immense doubt, you know that dream fulfillment is important you just may not be able to see how it's possible. You've got to understand that at times it can be hard for us to see the bigger picture because we are the frame. We need to stretch our thinking, stretch our beliefs, stretch our actions and stretch our Faith. *Faith is the substance of things hoped for and the evidence of things to seen.*

These things have special meaning because along our journeys faith will carry us through. If not faith in the Lord or whomever we deem to be God then surely faith in ourselves. Why would anyone do anything if they did not first believe that what they sought to achieve could in fact be done? You wouldn't try out for the football team or start a business if you didn't believe there was a reasonable chance of your genuine success. Faith in your ability to accomplish something and your ability to one day overcome is what will carry you through.

I'm asking you to reevaluate your plans, your dreams, your victories and your mistakes and gain a greater understanding of just where is it that you want to go. In this world you will find it hard to carry on, move on and go on without believing in something. It's up to you to find out what that is. Many people fail in life not because they aim to high and miss but because they aim to low, and hit!

Faith in God or in ourselves is about more than just belief. It is about concentrated action. It's about getting something done. It's about taking small steps, baby steps if need be till you get where you seek to go.

Faith without works is dead. One need not be a Christian to see truth in these words. Faith without works is nothing more than wishing. While I believe in the possibility of all things I do not expect at anytime to see the manifestation of the prayers we offer up to God simply by waiting on the couch and for blessings to rain down upon us mysteriously from the sky. It takes work, beyond hard work, an incredible ability to tolerate the tortuous terror of our times and press onward, forward until the time of our completing the great crossover, the blessed day of our fulfilled dreams.

In those moments what do you do when everything you have tried or believed wholeheartedly would work in fact does not work? What then? Do you give up? Quit and go the conventional path, the one traveled by most others? This is when prayer or meditation can help to restore balance and some type of order to the calamity that has become your life. During these times you need not panic, get all up and arms about situations that are in the past, can't be changed or that which you have no control over, especially other people. Ultimately, our fates are in our own hands. What becomes of your life is your choice. If you have made the decision, as I have, to not just have a dream but to go after it with all that you're able to muster from within, once such a journey has begun you must not give in to the pressure and stop your pursuit until you claim victory. There comes a moment when you know without saying that you have come too far to turn back now. There is a point of no return and as Les Brown says, it's not over until you win!

A CROSSOVER STORY

A Beautiful Tea Cup

According to your faith be it unto you.

–**Jesus Christ**, Mathew 9:29

When you've been after something for a long time you begin to think that any day now it will happen. You have worked toward your dreams so often for so long and you've revised your strategies over and over again, that you are now convinced that success or the big break you've been seeking is only just around the corner. All you've got to do is take another step forward, or do this one last thing. So you keep believing and you take this next step and do that one thing only to realize that there is yet another step to be taken, followed by another step. Soon even after years and years of constant, persistent effort you battle yet again the forces of doubt and the legions of negativity as you ponder what must be done to change your circumstances and gain greater momentum. Sometimes we become bogged down in the struggle, mired under a storm not knowing if it would ever pass and if you're not careful you will fool yourself into believing that the storm wont pass and will stifle your efforts and thwart your progress.

The trials we go through are not meant for our harm and will not last forever; they were meant to season us, to forge us into stronger beings preparing us for our rightful roles in the world. The difficulty and pain that make up the process of becoming more skilled, becoming a better person, of correcting past mistakes or making our dreams actually come true is necessary on many levels to force us to adapt to new hardships, to adopt stronger mindsets thus making us stronger human beings. It's very easy to get caught up in the crisis of the moment thinking that you will never overcome, believing that after all that has happened already that there is no way to overcome and that it's over. If you think like this, you will be neglecting the very important truth — it is not what happens that determines your life's future, it is what you do about what happens that makes all the difference.

Sometimes things have to happen for us to fully see how things might really be. We can be blinded by comforts that we take for granted and not grasp the blessings that surround us. Going through our trials and tribulations help us to tune into our own greater abilities of ingenuity under pressure, of rapid-fire creativity and problem solving genius under moments of duress. In this struggle so too exists the truth that we cannot grow without a challenge. If you yearn to have a multi-billion dollar company you had best be prepared for a challenge. You cannot get rich without a challenge. I'm trying to get rich at this very moment as you should be and you know what…it's a challenge! One of the keys to accomplishing this is to develop the wisdom to overcome the challenge.

To develop wisdom is to experience. It is to learn, to attempt to do things, to succeed and fail growing in your worldliness, understanding and in skill. We must proceed with our efforts knowing that for things to change, we must change. Our thoughts about our circumstances must change. Do not wish things were easier wish that you were better. With all your might, lean into greater understanding, striving to become a better self in all ways.

If you want to change your future and change your fortune, you've got to be open to new concepts and new ideas. The greatest concept to know, embrace and understand is that our thoughts can be manifested, that our goals can be met, that our dreams can come true. It's possible! Some people go year after year of not making their life better, of experiencing the same things over and over and over never progressing year after year because they don't know they have the power to make the change. There are those that just have not been told. They never got to the class. In their travels they somehow missed this vital piece of information, that it's possible, to change your future, to change your fortune, to change the world!

Like a pot being prepared by a potter, we start out unknowing, unwise and unprepared yet by undergoing the rigors and harsh treatment of being on the potters wheel, of feeling and living the setbacks, failures and disappointments that are a part of the dream fulfillment process we go on to improve and begin to shine throughout our lives as diamonds do amongst all other gems. I heard a story told once of an elderly couple who had been married many years and experienced great joy through antique shopping together. One day the couple came across the most exquisite teacup they had ever seen before. While the couple was admiring it the teacup suddenly spoke to them and said "I haven't always been this way you know. There was a time when nobody wanted me and I wasn't thought of as attractive. I was just a hard lump of clay. Then one day this potter came along and she began to shape me and mold me. I said 'hey! What are you doing? You're making me uncomfortable. This hurts! Leave me alone'."

The teacup then explained that to his surprise his requests went unanswered as the potter only smiled at him and said, "not yet." The teacup went on to explain "this potter just would not leave me be. She put me on a wheel and began to spin me around and around and I got the most dizzy I had ever been in my life, it was complete vertigo. When I calmed down a bit, I noticed that I had taken on a new shape. She formed me into this teacup. Then I thought she had finished when out of nowhere she put me into a furnace! It was so hot that I did not think I could stand it. When she came back to check on me and looked through the window of the furnace, she had a special look in her eye. I yelled 'let me out of here, it's too hot'! She said back to me 'not yet'. She finally took me out of the furnace, put me up on a shelf and left me alone. I thought to myself 'thank God that's over. Now I can go back to being my normal self'."

"To my surprise again the potter still was not done with me,' said the teacup. "She came and got me and began to paint me, changing me from gray to this magnificent blue. The paint was sticky, I thought I was going to choke, I told her to stop, but she said 'not yet'. Then she put me into a second oven, twice as hot as the first! This time I knew it was over. I screamed 'I'm not kidding, I can't take it! I'm going to die'! Finally, she opened the oven door, put me back on the shelf and I again began to cool and calm down."

"Now some weeks had passed and one day I came across a mirror and realized that I had become beautiful. I could not believe how much I had changed. I didn't look anything like that old lump of clay that I used to be. Now I am a beautiful teacup; valuable, expensive and unique when before no one used to want me. All because of what I went through, the molding, the pressure, the searing heat from my fires of affliction. What I thought was meant for my harm and destruction was actually destined to prepare and make me ready for my glorious future, which today is a part. You see, I once dreamed of having someone love and admire me and seek to take me home and make me a part of their family but I never thought it would happen.

During all the hardship, during my fires of affliction I became convinced that my dream would certainly never happen."

The nice elderly couple stood astonished by what they had heard, learned, and experienced from this teacup telling them the story from upon the shelf. They asked the teacup if he would like to come home with them and he tearfully responded, "That would be my dream finally come true. I most certainly would love to come home with you."

As the story goes that couple purchased the tea cup from the antiques dealer, the potter. She was overjoyed that someone had come to love her creation and wanted him to join their family. Like this teacup we at times will go through our own fires of afflictions. We too will go through and experience extreme difficulties that have untold benefits and allow us to grow up and persevere. To persevere means to continue onward in the face of hardships and difficulty, to overcome the anguish of our long suffering. If you do not first know within your own heart, and believe for yourself that what you aspire to become and seek to achieve can happen, come about and be brought into the real, then you will never take the needed steps to endure what must be endured and tolerate what must be tolerated so that you can walk into your glorious future and become the great and powerful figure you have it within yourself to be. As the lump of clay became the teacup, as the caterpillar becomes the butterfly, as the ugly duckling becomes the beautiful swan so too will you become your predestined great self if you walk and act with great belief. It's Possible!

DREAM FULFILLMENT EXERCISES

My Personal Interests & Concerns

Have you ever taken the time to consider just what your actual vision and values are? So many people are going day-to-day living uneventful and unfulfilling lives just getting by and accepting what comes along as part of the way that life just is. They never expect anything greater so they do not exert a greater effort thereby never achieving greatness. The fear of failure certainly is the most deadly for all entrepreneurs and would be history makers. If you desire to have a big oak tree, you are not going to have an oak tree until you first start with and carefully nurture a very small acorn. There is something in your life right now that can cause you to be a history maker. God has destined you to leave your mark on this generation. You are not supposed to come and go and no one ever know that you were here. When your time is up the world should look back and say, "Wow!" He left a legacy of hope" "she left a trail of support." Your dream may be big and your resources may be small but if you will use what you have you will find a way to multiply your access and to multiply your resources. Never has there been a greater time to ask yourself some very critical questions so that you can learn more and contribute more to the place you live. The blessings are out there. Seek and ye shall find. You have the power!

Place an X next to the choices that you feel most passionate about. This will help you further develop a crystallized view of your unique dream. Of course if I've left something out that you feel strongly about and you feel needs to be added to this list, then by all means, write that down. This exercise is about you discovering what's important about you.

Vision & Values

__ Achievement	__ Empathy	__ Patriotism
__ Accessibility	__ Faith	__ Peace
__ Community	__ Family	__ Preservation
__ Compassion	__ Freedom	__ Quality
__ Cooperation & Collaboration	__ Generosity	__ Security
	__ Humility	__ Self-Respect
__ Courage	__ Independence	__ Service
__ Creativity	__ Innovation	__ Spirituality
__ Determination	__ Integrity	__ Teamwork
__ Dignity	__ Knowledge	__ Technology
__ Diversity	__ Loyalty	__ Tradition

Topics of Interest

As you did for your vision and values do the same for your topics of interests, and by all means write your own areas of interest that I have not included or that comes to your mind as you complete this exercise.

- __ Animals
- __ Anti-Racism
- __ Child Welfare
- __ Civil rights/Social Justice
- __ Community Development
- __ Crime Prevention/Legal Assistance
- __ Disease/Disorder prevention
- __ Domestic Violence
- __ Drugs and Alcohol Recovery
- __ Education
- __ Employment
- __ Entrepreneurship
- __ Environment/Nature
- __ Food / Nutrition / Agriculture
- __ General / Rehabilitative Health
- __ Cultural Development
- __ Housing / Shelter
- __ Humanities
- __ Human Services
- __ International Relations
- __ Libraries
- __ Medical Research
- __ Mental Health
- __ Museums
- __ Music
- __ Neighborhood improvement
- __ Performing Arts
- __ Poverty
- __ Public Safety / Disaster Relief
- __ Recreation /Athletics
- __ Religion
- __ Technology
- __ Visual Arts
- __ Youth Development
- __ Public Policy
- __ International Relations
- __ Music
- __ Space Exploration

Beneficiaries of your efforts and work

__ Adolescents
__ Blacks
__ The Unemployed
__ Animals
__ Immigrants
__ Men / Boys
__ Refugees
__ Veterans
__ Native Americans
__ Latinos
__ Asians
__ Pacific Islanders
__ Rural Farmers
__ The Disabled
__ Gay / Lesbian / Bisexual / Transgendered
__ Senior Citizens
__ Young Adults
__ Women / Girls
__ Threatened / Indigenous Populations

Your dreams are a part of the everlasting essence of you. Your dreams ARE you. You are your dreams. Your dreams are important. They are not things that you should work on from time to time and when you get busy or distracted you put them back in the drawer until you have time later.

Fulfilling Goal Setting and Achievement

I've spoken a lot about the power of having a dream, nurturing it and bringing it to life and if you do not currently have something that you're living for it may seem too easy for me to sit here and tell you to develop your dream when you may not even have one or ever thought about it. Now is the time for you to start taking the initial steps of first identifying just what it is that you want to do. The beginning of completing the great crossover, of taking the intangible and forcing it into the real, of making the invisible APPEAR, begins now! By the time you complete these exercises you will have created a feeling that is so great, so compelling that you just wont be able to avoid taking action today. As you take these steps a vision will start to take shape in your mind and the affection you have for this vision will demand that you work to bring it into existence. Four areas to be covered are:

- Personal Development Goals
- Career/Business/Economic Goals
- Adventure Goals
- Contribution Goals

For all of these areas you will brainstorm for moments of time and write down all you can think of. The most important thing is that you allow the ideas to flow and the pen must move and dance with the pad while you DO NOT censor yourself. This is the chance for everything you've ever wanted and every fantasy to come out. Just ask yourself "What would I want for myself in my life if I could have it any way I wanted it? What would I go for if I were certain to succeed and could not fail? This part is getting the inspiration out. Worry later about how it will all work. For each of the goals listed you will spend 5 minutes writing and listing all of the different goals that you have for yourself in each specific area. Once this is complete you will spend an additional minute or so placing a timeline by each goal that you've expressed. This is the action of deciding when it is you plan to accomplish the expressed goals.

Start with your **Personal Development Goals**. With your notebook get into a mindset of total faith and complete expectation, that all you aim to do, you will do, that all that you aim to have, you will have. You can now get ANYTHING YOU WANT! This is now the time for feeling that wonderful feeling of freedom, of having a life without limits. Thinking of your own personal growth, write down everything you want to accomplish in your life. What languages do you want to learn or how many degrees do you want to have? What addictions or limitations do you want to overcome? What relationships do you want to build or repair? How enlightened would you like to become? These can be short term or long-term goals. They can be things you do 30 years from now and things you can do tomorrow. Take five minutes and do not stop writing at anytime while listing all the personal development ideas and wants that you would like to accomplish for yourself. Do not just read this but DO THIS! Life does not change by reading alone; it is the actions taken after the reading of wisdom that inspire and forge new futures.

Take another minute and go back to put a timeline by each goal that you've expressed. This is the action of deciding when it is you plan to accomplish the written goals. Again, it doesn't matter at this moment how you're going to do what you're destined to do, just write when you want to achieve them by. The action of deciding when we want to achieve something puts in motion conscious and subconscious forces that aide in our making dreams come true. Now if you are committed to attainting a goal within one year just write a 1 next to it. If the goal is for three years write a 3. If it's for five years write a 5. For twenty write a 20.

Now for your **Career/Business/Economic goals**. Spend five minutes writing nonstop about your goals in all these areas. What are you investment goals? What does your financial future look like? If you've never thought of it in real terms now is the time to do so. Often all we think of is wishing we had more money because we don't have enough right now. It's time for specifics. How much money do you want to make in a year or in your lifetime? What professional breakthroughs would you like to make? What type of legacy will you leave? How strong of an impact do you want to have? When you complete this action again take a moment and place the times you would like to achieve this by.

Next, your **Adventure Goals** — your fantastic fun goals. Once again spend at least 5 minutes on a new sheet of paper brainstorming about what you would like to build, purchase or create. What are the things that would offer complete and lasting enjoyment for you? Would you like to own your home on the beach? A movie studio? Start your own music school? Sail a yacht in the tropics? Scuba dive in the Bermuda triangle, and live to tell the tale? Create your own indoor paintball/monster truck obstacle course? Let your imagination go free. You get to have whatever you want on this list. Nothing can be wrong here. Now put a timeline on these goals showing when you will achieve each of them.

Lastly, your **Contribution Goals**. This is your opportunity to leave your mark on the world and is really the most important goal of all. This is a chance to truly make a difference in people's lives. Perhaps you want to build a school in a poor country as I do or develop unique funding for underprivileged children to attend prekindergarten programs. Maybe you yearn to adopt a child, clean up the environment or mentor juvenile offenders.

You have now written down a long list of goals, visions and plans that you would like to see come into existence. Spend five minutes writing nonstop about your goals in each of these areas. After this is complete pick the most important 1-year goal in each category and now write a paragraph with all the compelling reasons why you will complete this goal in one year. Think of the goals that offer tremendous excitement if they were to be completed this year. Something that inspires you, that gets you up early and keeps you up into the late hours. The thing that if happened would certainly give your life special meaning and significance in unique and important ways. Take these goals and for two minutes write down why you are utterly committed to achieving this goal within one year. Why is this vision compelling to you? What will you gain by accomplishing it? What would you miss out on if you do not achieve it? Your reasons must be strong enough to force you to follow through with the necessary actions consistently and enthusiastically. Take some time and do this now!

From now on at least twice a day think of and emotionally enjoy the experience of achieving each one of your highly valued goals. Each time you do this you need to create more emotional joy as to better see, hear and feel yourself living your dream. This continuous focus will literally create a mental pathway between where you are and where you want to go. Because of this intense conditioning, you will find yourself feeling a sense of absolute certainty that you will achieve your desires. This feeling of certainty will translate into a quality of actions that will lead in fact to your greatest desires being made real! This book is proof in and of itself!

Self Discovery Questions:

What can I improve or change in the issues I care about most

_____

_____

_____

How can my giving support improvement or change?

_____

_____

_____

What are the grand dreams within your mind's eye and how will you will make them even greater?

_____

_____

_____

What am I passionate about changing in the world?

_____

_____

_____

What can I improve or change in the issues I care about most?

_____

_____

_____

How can my giving support improve or change?

_____

_____

_____

The time line for my actions ahead are?

_____

_____

_____

Your Personal Mission Statement

The mission statement represents the core of your commitment to your vision of an improved and greater self and community. When you are preparing your mission statement, remember to make it clear, succinct and to incorporate meaningful and measurable criteria while approaching it from a grand scale. The preparation of your mission statement is a time for reflection upon your values, areas of interests and goals. Use the exercises on the following pages as a basis for ongoing considerations including discussions with your family, friends, and colleagues. You can use my own personal mission statement as a model to guide the formation of your own.

Example: *My mission is to advance the broader human conversation for the betterment of positive social progress. My purpose is to assist and contribute to the evolutionary enlightenment process taking place throughout human history; to leave a lasting legacy of love by alleviating human suffering, poverty and indignity while mitigating the forces of greed, racism and elitism.*

_____

_____

_____

_____

_____

_____

_____

_____

_____

Five things you can do to start your own business now:

1. Develop a concept

2. Believe its possible

3. Be bold in your approach and take MASSIVE ACTION

4. Ask for help

5. Pray/meditate/focus on it all day and all night!

Dream Fulfillment Model:

It's important that you are able to associate as many powerful visions and pleasant emotions as possible with your dreams and the idea of them being made real. You may develop a big lofty dream or already have one you may only now be starting the process by which to craft a roadmap of how you will make your imaginations manifest in our physical world. The journey that is dream fulfillment and the roads that we will traverse will certainly not come with any map and even if it did X would not mark the spot. We must rely on our instincts. Success leaves clues and we must study and use the experience and examples of our peers and historical heroes to illuminate our own path to a glorious future. Provided below is a model for you to use as you consider your dreams/visions/plans and how best to go about accomplishing them.

We start with your dreams first. You've got to first have a vision of something that you would like to see made real, of something that you would like to see occur. When you develop the basic concept for this vision, you must then associate great feelings of pleasure with the visual image of those occurrences and now infuse those emotional visions with unwavering confidence and belief. You must actually believe with a great certainty that what you seek to have happen for you will inevitably come about once you take the necessary actions. Now that you have established such belief, the potential for greater achievements and grander success scenarios begins to become plausible in your mind. What you once thought was impossible, now appears attainable; difficult and tough but possible and you're aware of your capability. Now an inspirational jolt will take place within your mind and within your heart and spirit because if that which makes your heart most happy can inevitably occur you will be unable to not take MASSIVE ACTION that will inevitably lead to positive RESULTS.

Experiencing the results of taking passionate persistent MASSIVE ACTION will further spurn greater belief and forge greater and grander dreams within your minds eyes that you will take even greater MASSIVE ACTION to bring about greater results!

Potential >>>>>>>>>>>>>>>>>>>>>Massive Action
^   ^
^   ^
^   ^

Belief <<<<<<<<<<<<<<<<<<<<<<<<<<<<<<

BONUS CHAPTER

It's Never Too Late

If our young men miscarry in their first enterprises they lose all heart. If the young merchant fails, men say he is ruined. College graduates are considered a failure if they are not installed in an office within one year afterwards in the cities or suburbs of Boston or New York. The supple person who in turn tries all the professions, who teams it, farms it, peddles it, keeps a school, preaches, edits a newspaper, goes to congress, buys a township and so forth, in successive years, and always like a cat, falls on his feet, is worth a hundred of these city dolls.

— **Ralph Waldo Emerson**

Only in death is it ever too late for your dreams and desired accomplishments to come to life. At that point it's in God's hands and will be his decision to make. Until that day, as long as there is breath in your lungs you have a fighting chance to realize your aspirations and make real all that you've longed for.

The best example of this in my own life is the recommendation from my own family, the release of this very book, (FINALLY), and the completion of the Ambassador Trek program and connecting young people with other cultures while building bridges of success across the world. From my earliest days all I've ever wanted was to do something magnificent, memorable and genuinely beneficial to a large number of people. These days I think of it as a desire to do great works upon the earth by helping people in a meaningful way that actually matters in a capacity that will have my time on Earth remembered throughout history. I've waited my whole life to do something powerfully important that would allow my name to live on.

My greatest dream in life is to do something for our Black Diaspora; something so meaningful, so important, so very powerful that I may be remembered forever for the legacy of love that I left for others. I want to become a man who is remembered for how bravely I fought for justice and truth and for how fiercely I loved my fellow human being. I want for school children in foreign lands, hundreds of years in the future, in their time to know what it was that I did in my own time and why it mattered. My private thoughts of this are what make my heart most happy. This is my deepest prayer. This is what my soul cries about to God for a blessing. This is my dream. This is what I expect to crossover into. While it has taken me a long time, while I've failed more than a few times, history and God proves that IT'S NEVER TOO LATE. IT'S NEVER TOO LATE for me and it's never too late for you.

The biggest task I've ever undertaken other than graduating from college is The Omaha Ambassador Trek. All of my passions, personal interests talents and skill sets combined to become this great effort to travel to Malawi, East Africa with area high school students and build a school. I have tried, prayed and have done everything under the sun that my mind could conceive that might bring this vision of mine to fulfillment. And to this very day nothing has worked…yet. No mine to fulfillment. And to this very day nothing has worked. No matter how great of an idea I thought something was, no matter how much effort I exerted, no matter how much blood, sweat and tears I shed, I just could not bring this vision to fruition where I was. So here I am in Conway, Arkansas writing this bonus chapter for a book that I had long envisioned being published many months ago but as it is for me so too it is *NEVER* too late for you.

This Omaha Ambassador Trek has been long in the making. So long has it been floating between the planning and fundraising stage and back and forth again and again that there was a time when I had thought this never would actually occur. The delay of goals and desires year after year after year can very easily distract one from the work that must be done. If you're not careful you may become more focused on what hasn't worked and what may be blocking you instead of recognizing the tools you *DO* have at your disposal and the advancements that you've yet made.

I open this bonus chapter with a magnificent quotation from Ralph Waldo Emerson because it is relevant not only to the title of this chapter; IT'S NEVER TOO LATE, but also because I relate to it personally. I myself over the course of my young life have tried my hands at many things as one of my personal heroes, John Brown had done. I've bravely ventured into the uncharted wilderness of business and can say with certainty the road to success and significant achievement is never without setbacks or disappointment. Though reaching success at the summit of this mountain with perseverance *IS* possible. This book, the *P.R.O.G.R.E.S.S. to P.O.W.E.R.* program, the Omaha and Arkansas Ambassador Trek are my latest attempt of business ownership and creation under the banner of Global Renaissance, LLC. Having tried and failed in business before is in no way a deterrent for me to try yet again. The greatest teachers a person has are often their most recent mistakes. For all of life's greats, success has been born out of failure.

It is common for the story of Abraham Lincoln to be told and retold concerning his many failures and relatively few successes on his way toward his ultimate achievement of becoming President of the United States of America.

A common list of Abraham Lincoln's failures (along with a few successes) are as follows:

- 1831 - Lost his job
- 1832 - Defeated in run for Illinois State Legislature
- 1833 - Failed in business
- 1834 - Elected to Illinois State Legislature (success)
- 1835 - Sweetheart died
- 1836 - Had nervous breakdown
- 1838 - Defeated in run for Illinois House Speaker
- 1843 - Defeated in run for nomination for U.S. Congress
- 1846 - Elected to Congress (success)
- 1848 - Lost re-nomination
- 1849 - Rejected for land officer position
- 1854 - Defeated in run for U.S. Senate
- 1856 - Defeated in run for nomination for Vice President
- 1858 - Again defeated in run for U.S. Senate
- 1860 - Elected President (success)

The most important lesson from this as I see it is the ability to continue no matter the set back, time and time again until ultimate victory is rightfully achieved. It is stick-to-it-ative-ness combined with the blessings of an unwavering faith in God, faith in yourself, faith in your abilities or faith in something that will allow you to be successful. Just like the old spiritual song "We Shall Overcome," you too shall overcome so long as you continue forever forward, forever learning as you forever strive for the realization of your dreams.

Depending upon who you are and your own history and philosophical belief system this probably sounds easier than it can be done. But that is conscious positive decision making. By making the choice to continue onward, by deciding to go at the process of goal attainment again and again in spite of whatever negatives may have happened in the past, what you're doing is choosing to NOT become One of the stagnant majority. I'm talking about the stagnant majority of all human beings who never go on to live their dreams, the stagnant majority who never make it to the mountain top for fear they have much longer to go when really they are nearly there. If only they would have just kept taking steps, baby steps if need be they would eventually someday, someway lead to the summit of the mountain. If after a devastating loss for United States Senate Abraham Lincoln had just thrown his hands up and quit politics because he didn't want to face another possible bout with insanity or public rejection and humiliation, he never would have become president of the United States of America and therefore never would have waged war upon the south and therefore never would have issued the Emancipation Proclamation that was meant to free Blacks in America and end slavery. Think about how a decision to quit in this instance would have affected not just our national culture but the world. It could be argued that President Barack Obama in 2009 never would have taken his oath of office using Abraham Lincoln Bible or been president at all for that matter had Mr. Lincoln not had the stick-to-it-ative-ness to see past the setbacks, fight through his failures and stay at it until his personal dreams were fulfilled. Especially now that it's known that President Barack Obama is directly related to the very 1st African slave of this country, Mr. John Punch.

It's the story of most peoples' lives to give up after a few instances of trouble, to quit after some setbacks and that fatal decision is what places them among the stagnant. I'm asking and suggesting to you that you walk away from the stagnant majority. Walk away from the destructive action of choosing the negative over the positive. Walk away from a dreary defeatist attitude. Walk away from the stagnant majority. Don't go where they go! Don't do what they do! Walk away today! When you walk away from the negativity of the stagnant majority you gain power over your obstacles, you are thereby choosing to adopt and practice a whole new language of positive action. This is a language that the whole world can understand. A language that transcends cultural differences, transcends national boundaries, transcends all differences that exist between all the human beings who make up our world because everyone understands what unyielding tenacity is. We all stand up, recognize and take notice when a person, any person overcomes incredible odds, personal setbacks and limitations and past failures and go on to final victory. It doesn't matter who you are; William Kampwamba, Sylvester Stallone, Abraham Lincoln or Joseph G. Smith, II, or YOU! In this great and grand wonderful world of ours, anything and everything is possible, all you've got to do is try.

Whatever your dreams, no matter your goals, in spite of everything bad that may have happened and in the face of all the negative nay-sayers and their nasty forecasts of an unfortunate future, in spite of it all, if you dare to keep dreaming, keep pressing, keep pushing, keep pulling, keep knowing beyond knowing that you can do it, surely God will help you through it. Yes, You Can! IT'S NEVER TOO LATE.

A CROSSOVER EXIT

Reanna Profit and the SPRANIMALS

Kindness is a language that a deaf person can hear and a blind person can see.

— **Mark Twain**

The Great Crossover is the completion of the journey from dreaming to dream fulfillment. It is the culmination of the many moments one spends dreaming, wishing, working and waiting for this great dream, to step out of its birth place of intangibility and into the world of our experienced existence. Anyone with a great thing to achieve is at work almost always to make real this Great Crossover for them. I am always at work to make real and bring about the Ambassador Trek and *P.R.O.G.R.E.S.S. to P.O.W.E.R.* programs without having even done it yet. Just the thought of it coming true is what fills my spirit with joy and makes my heart most happy. Even when I'm not working on it my mind is forever engaged in thoughts of it and plans to accomplish it, asking myself the important questions about what I need to get farther down the road. My mind's eye cannot turn away from it.

I hope this book has encouraged you to overcome your obstacles and to continue on to your unique level of greatness. Completing The Great Crossover for me goes beyond the boundaries of any nation impacted by the success of The Ambassador Trek and beyond the confines of my personal physical being and soul. To Crossover into greatness means that I must aide and assist others throughout the dream fulfillment process, particularly my own family and specifically my niece, Reanna Profit. I love my niece very much and when I told her about my dream and efforts to build a school in Africa she was excited and immediately wanted to help, she just didn't know how. Before I get to this part of the story I have to first offer some background on her and her interests as to how it relates.

One day, not long ago (June 14, 2012), I was in Wal-Mart buying some things as I often am and my niece happened to come along with me. She followed me aisle through aisle as I had come for health food, fitness related products and the usual knick knacks. We had a great conversation about things of life in general. We talked about school and her friends. As we walked and talked we somehow made our way to the toy aisle, her "favorite aisle," she alerted me personally to. I view the toy aisle as the biggest waste of space in the store and as completely fraudulent as television advertisers have become masters of subliminally ordering children to barrage and cajole parents and adults to spend precious hard earned dollars on things these children do not need yet have become convinced is paramount for their continued existence. For Reanna, the things she "needs" are dolls. I laugh unto myself as I write this because she is so funny when talking about these new monster high school dolls and her "need" for Draculaura, a doll of Dracula's daughter. The doll was $22.97. Of course Draculaura needs to have a car and that also was 22.97. I love my niece and want her to have the things she wants but I wasn't able to spend 50 bucks on dolls and accessories. I told her that she didn't need those things. Our conversation followed, "Yes, I do," Reanna said.

"No, you don't. You're only asking for these things because television told you to want them," I responded.

She said, "Television didn't tell me to want them; I tell myself I want them."

I countered, "Yes, television does actually tell you to want these things. You spend all day taking orders from Nick Jr. and the Disney channel and now that we're in Wal-mart, you're following those orders." As you can imagine this went on for some time.

I took this back and forth dialogue as an opportunity to speak to Reanna about Entrepreneurship, to tell her about how and why instead of buying dolls for 22.97 that she should start making her own dolls and selling them. This way she is putting money in her pocket instead of taking money out and handing it to someone else. I went on to share the inspirational stories I knew of young entrepreneurs, of teenage millionaires and pre teens who are the creators of wonderful works that are purchased and enjoyed by millions. I shared with her the subject of a crossover story within this book, Mr. Arion Rashad and his comic creations of MII Toons. I told my niece that she could do the same thing, that she could become the creator of something great and sell them and make money.

We made our way from the toy aisle to the crafts aisle and continued to talk. She told me that she could make her own dolls/toys out of some simple craft items and I bought them for her. I asked her if she would like to make some toys or something similar and then after selling them to use some of the money to build a school in Africa. She said yes. She wants to help people so why not.

After even more talking, planning, strategizing and prototype development the *SPRANIMALS* were born. Very simple in their nature they are painted wooden animals sitting on springs. To assist with the Ambassador Trek and other programs of my business New World Vision Incorporated, a percentage of the purchase price of each *SPRANIMAL* will be donated to the materials needed to build the 3 room school house in Malawi, East Africa and Nicaragua Central America.

Reanna Profit is an 11 year old entrepreneurial newbie. A young southern gal raised with love and respect for herself, her family and the Lord. She is a 6th grader with grandiose dreams of becoming a surgeon. At the heart of her interest is her natural desire to help and be good to people and leave a legacy of greatness for herself. As she tells it, "I want to be a doctor because I could find a cure for cancer so people won't have it anymore. So people won't die from it. I would cure all the diseases so people could live healthy and happy lives, because that is the right thing to do. Plus, I want to be famous and known for something good."

This is what legacy creation is in the mind of an 11 year old. The story of my niece and the *SPRANIMALS* is my own personal tale of crossing over from a whole other viewpoint. I aim for this school we build and this book to help, inspire, motivate, and uplift others in their efforts to make their dreams come true for them. This is what I seek to have happen for the boys and girls that attend our school. This is what I aim to occur for you, the reader of this book. I especially seek these things for my own family and what better way for me to complete these tasks than with my own niece. To see my niece work from the idea stage and into the business sales stage would be a great crossover of the entrepreneurial and dream fulfillment process, as well as a crossing over for me having had a direct impact in helping another accomplish this.

SPRANIMALS are animal creations resting on springs that bounce. They are fun, lovable animal creations. Keeping in line with her own ideals of selflessness Reanna said "If I sold the *SPRANIMALS* and didn't do something for others that would be selfish. People need a school so they can grow up smart. My *SPRANIMAL* creations being used to raise money for building a school is a really good thing. I want to give money to charity because it's fun. People who are poor need stuff and it we don't help them, bad things happen."

If you buy a SPRAINIMAL
you will be helping advance The Ambassador Trek program
and making my dreams come true.

— Reanna Profit

Even a mistake may turn out to be the one thing necessary to a worthwhile achievement.

—Henry Ford

Why I Build

It is easier to build strong children than to repair broken men.

— **Frederick Douglas**

I was asked not long ago the question, "what is it that you want to do"? For me, this question has many answers. I yearn to do so very many things, all with great purpose and meaning. I feel that what I want most to do with my life is to help others in a very large way, in a way that is larger than my dreams appear within my heart. Somewhere along the way I've developed a zeal for creating and leaving a legacy. I want to make and leave the world better upon my exit than when I found it at the time of my birth. A legacy is that which we bless others with for a time when we will be unable to hear the praise and laughter of those we have blessed through the trials of our labor.

It is now, in our time and through our sweat and labor that we praise and honor those who have provided what we enjoy today; their legacy as we engage with due diligence to create and leave our own for descendents who have not yet come but are indeed on their way. I have a deep and burning passion to show, teach and convey to our younger generation the value of service toward one another. This is why I build. With your help, youth of Nebraska and Arkansas will also build.

We will work to build a school in Malawi, East Africa and we work to build a school in Nicaragua, Central America because we desire to build a future world that is greater than today's world. The Bible says that good men leave an inheritance to their children's children and that is why we build. A good person takes care of his family and loves his fellow man and that is why we build.

Building these schools, building strong minds within the halls of these schools that will go on to build great inventions and provide a bountiful blessing for others is my dream. This has been my dream for a very long time and I have an intensely stubborn faith that The Great Crossover be made and dreams may come true with visions taking real shape. When a dream so wonderful in its nature has affixed itself unto ones heart as mine has done, the dream itself takes on a life all its own becoming a living, breathing, feeling and uniquely real entity. Albeit intangible, this dream refuses to submit to the dormant realm of mere possibility and will fight like hell to join us all in our existing place of reality. This is what The Omaha Ambassador Trek and The Arkansas Ambassador Trek are; living breathing, feeling entities, albeit intangible for the moment, refusing to remain dormant.

These dreams of mine have long been printed indelibly on my mind and within my heart and this why I build.

I am motivated to complete The Omaha and Arkansas Ambassador Treks in part because of my Christian faith. I really do believe that in this life of ours and within this world we temporarily occupy, Gods work must truly become our own. I want to live a good life as a good man. I believe that the manifestation of Gods work conducted through us are within the reality one creates in service of the poor, the sick and the enslaved and oppressed. In human history it is our personal acts of selflessness and love that have brought Gods grace to the many and will do so again in our broken world mired in tragedy. Instilling the vision and values of well doing in the minds of American youth, this is why I build.

I believe that Christians, Muslims, Hindus, Atheists and all others are NOT diametrically opposed to one another. Though we may have different systems of belief, we all share the same world, we all breathe the same air, we all cherish our children's future and we all are mortal. For these reasons I resolutely believe we should all be-constantly engaged in the noble actions of becoming more dedicated world changers. We are not just passing through this world. I believe we were placed here to make a difference. We could do worse than to think in these terms.

I, for one, chose to joyfully take up the glorious banner of positive global leadership and train our youth to carry the banner of service and humane love. In our sometimes shameless, materialistic world of mindless consumerism we could be focused upon keeping up with the Joneses and being among the first to purchase the newest gadget but I believe it to be time better spent for one to instead be making the world more Godly and just through the service of others. My name is Joseph G. Smith, II, and this is why I build.

*A man is but the product of his thoughts.
What he thinks, he becomes.*

— Mohandas K. Gandhi

The Global Renaissance Movement

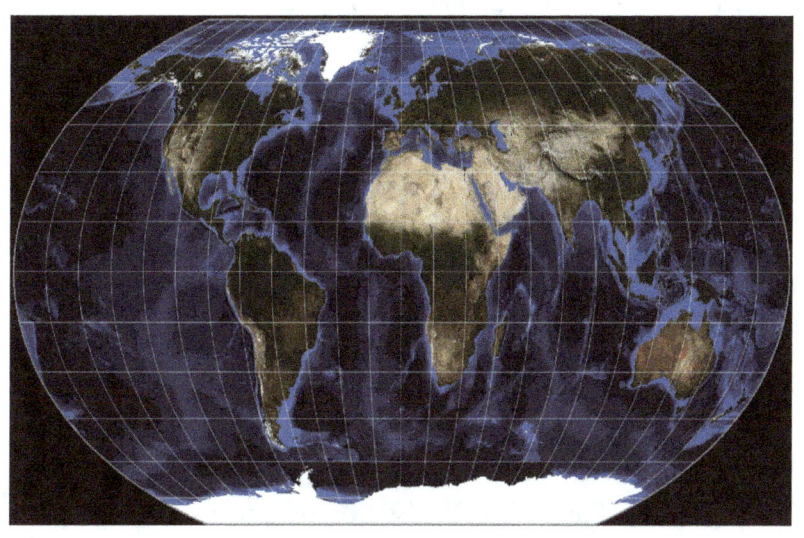

*Those who love peace
must learn to organize as effectively as
those who love war.*

— Martin Luther King Jr.

The Global Renaissance Movement is the combined energies and actions of all those who look out upon the global landscape and recognize that we as a people, as a human species, can do better, that we can be more than we are and have more than we've got, but only through massive positive action. This is a movement to remake the world. It is a global movement to promote, fight for and bring about world peace, freedom and friendship among all the worlds citizens. Taking massive positive action is necessary for the creation of the better planet all of us want and badly need. Recently one of my students, Carter, commented in class, "You know what, Mr. J, the world really is a messed up place." I agreed with him that the world is indeed a messed up place, but it doesn't have to be. Each day that we are blessed with oxygen in our lungs and the opportunity of a new day, that is a chance to get it right, to have more and contribute more than the day before. For me this is my chance to be a better man today than I was yesterday, an attitude and approach to life I teach my students.

We all have our own unique role to play throughout the never-ending human story. Everyone has his or her own passions and creative abilities. Teaching kids about the positive path of business is MY role. Inspiring my own peer group to commit acts of public service is MY role. Telling the world my truth, that EVERYTHING IS POSSIBLE, is MY role. What's yours?

Acting upon my truth that everything is indeed possible, I have brought to life The Global Renaissance Movement, a means of my connecting with others who share my philosophy; those who really mean it when they say they want to change the world. With technology and strategic partnerships such as my working with Non-Government Organization Build On, incredible goals are attainable such as the building of a primary school in Malawi and giving my students from Omaha, Nebraska the global engagement opportunities and international travel experience that they need.

The students of Malawi will get a new school and our American students will have their eyes opened to realities that they had not previously known to exist. Friendships will be forged, memories will be made, lessons will be learned, yet most importantly two groups of people, from two different hemispheres, from two different world experiences will have the fortunate opportunity to meet and befriend one another and through the shared labor of school construction, lives will be transformed and our world will be changed.

This book you are holding contributes to the construction materials of the school itself. The Omaha Ambassador Trek at this moment in time is my biggest dream that I WILL see become a great reality. This reality is the beginning of The Global Renaissance Movement, the connection for the first time of people who already are making a difference in their own communities, those who always wanted to change the world but never knew how, and those who are newly awakened to the realities of our world both good and bad and now possess a sudden desire for participation in a way that will actually matter. For the first time these groups of people can join together, learn about one another, support each other and see the results of their efforts.

I invite you to join us. JOIN THE MOVEMENT!

To Support The Global Renaissance Movement:

- Request for your organization a speaker from our *Global Renaissance Bureau of Speakers*
- Purchase a copy of this book, *The Crossover: Making Your Biggest Dreams Your Greatest Reality*, for your friend, child or student. This is a quality book for all people of all ages.
- Subscribe to our newsletter, *The Renaissance*
- Make a direct Contribution to *The Omaha Ambassador Trek* and the strategic visions of *The Global Renaissance Movement* at: GoFundMe.com/TheOmahaAmbassadorTrek

A portion of each copy of this book sold directly contributes to the construction materials used to build the primary school in Malawi as part of **The Omaha Ambassador Trek**. At this moment in time this is my biggest dream that I WILL see become a great reality. This reality is the beginning of **The Global Renaissance Movement!** I invite you to join this movement and help us to remake the world.

EIPILOGUE

The Arkansas Ambassador Trek

For someone, the light at the end of the tunnel is YOU!

— Joseph G. Smith, II

It seems extremely weird for me to say or write the words, The Arkansas Ambassador Trek. That's because for more than a couple years just about everything I've done has centered around The OMAHA Ambassador Trek which is the title of the prologue chapter of this book. I first came to Omaha, Nebraska after graduating from Wayne State College in Wayne, Nebraska. I'd lived in Omaha for the last 7 years. Naturally, me being the man that I am, I sought to make a difference in the community in which I lived so right away I was always looking to be a part of a progressive effort to make life better in Omaha, to positively influence kids in Omaha, to leave my own positive legacy in Omaha. I joined the local NAACP, I worked as an independent motivational speaker, I taught my own original enrichment program through the Omaha Public School system, I became part of more independent business initiatives than I can remember and finally I came upon the Non-Government Organization Build On and became almost immediately enthralled within their

Ambassador Trek program, the effort to build a 3 room school house in a country that needs schools. Right away I just knew that this was the program that I'd been looking for, the opportunity to do great work abroad that wasn't long in its time commitment (I considered joining the Peace Corps but didn't want to be gone for two years).

In my case with the countries that have active programs available I selected Mali, West Africa (In light of recent and dangerous developments in Mali, school building efforts there through the Build on Ambassador Trek program has been suspended. All work now is shifted to Malawi, East Africa and Nicaragua). I chose an African nation for several reasons. First, Being a Black man in love with history I always wanted to visit the African continent as all world history begins there. Second, since even to this very day I've never traveled to another nation, a country within the African continent made the most sense. Third, The Ambassador Trek as I envision it is an opportunity to connect African-Americans with Africans. Part of the challenges facing African-Americans in my view is a lack in knowledge of self and being disconnected from their heritage. I firmly believe that Black American youth having the opportunity to spend 15 days in Africa, living and fellowshipping with their African brothers and sisters, engaged in a most noble endeavor that is building a school, would do much for the attitude and aptitude development of those young people. I believe whole heartedly that the terrible dropout rate and awful violence problems we face can be mitigated if the youth are afforded opportunities to expand their global perspective and recognize the greatness they possess.

However much has changed since I began writing this book nearly 1 year ago. Life has seen fit for me to leave the city of Omaha and while my body is no longer present my heart is still there. I now reside in Conway, Arkansas and have been an Arkansan for roughly 7 weeks now at the time of writing this epilogue (June 13, 2012) and because of this move I've had to rethink some things. I had to reconfigure all that I've worked on as everything has been about The

OMAHA Ambassador Trek but I no longer live in Omaha, so the question had become what to do about this? I'd been asking myself questions such as, should I try to conduct the Omaha Ambassador Trek from Conway? Should I just cancel the Omaha Ambassador Trek all together and just work toward what I would call the *ARKANSAS* Ambassador Trek? To do that I would have to rearrange everything! I didn't and I don't want to do that because it would mean basically throwing out all that I'd done thus far with the Omaha Dream Team and my website OmahasFinest.com. It would be a pain to my heart and soul if I had to do that so I will not. I've come too far to turn back now. I've done too much to just turn my back on the people who have helped me, the businesses who have advertised with me and everyone who has believed in me. So with that said after much prayer and deliberation and advice from a pastor who doesn't even know I was listening I have decided to conduct both, The Omaha Ambassador Trek AND The Arkansas Ambassador Trek!

    I have come to know, realize and believe that our dreams no matter what they may be, should they be delayed, they are not denied. They shall not be denied so long as we are willing to put in the work and believe even when times become unbelievable. I've had to change things up more than a few times regarding fundraising and team membership and overall strategy. I offer permanent advertising for sale on my websites OmahasFinest.com and ArkansasFinest.org as well as portions of the purchase price of this book as well as a percentage of all speaking fees toward the vision that is The Omaha and Arkansas Ambassador Treks. Other ideas and funding plans may take shape and if they do you will be among the first to know, until then this is the plan and I humbly request your support.

    My vision to have a great impact upon the world stage neither starts nor ends with The Omaha and Arkansas Ambassador Trek. It seems at times that my mind houses more dreams than it can contain yet still I dream on and on. I yearn to encourage people, youth especially, to recognize their greatness but to do something *meaningful* with that greatness. I write a lot in this book about leaving a lasting legacy of love, a legacy that will be felt and experienced for generations beyond our own, but what does this really mean? It means to educate yourself about the *REAL* world that we live in and learn to associate your passions in the blessed area of problem solving and do something *meaningful* for someone else. What I seek to help people realize is that life is not about you or me the individual, life is about *WE* the collective. When we help others reach their levels we inevitably help ourselves.

Global Renaissance, LLC is firmly dedicated to the noble misssion of poverty reduction, the alleviation of human suffering and the elimination of racism, sexism and elitism, the real scourges that plague the world we live in. Through the purchase of this book you have directly aided in those causes and I thank you. Through the purchase of this book you have helped me to make my great crossover and I am grateful. It is doubtful that you can know the true depths of my thanks and how my soul stands in awe at the most majestic blessing you have given me this day.

So I close saying thank you, offering my prayers unto God for you and your family and I leave you with a most sincere request to please do contact me if there is something I can do for you or an effort or a cause that I may assist you in. We are all most certainly in this together. I leave you now saying thank you, I love you and God Bless you!

Joseph G. Smith, II

Thank Yous and Blessings

This book has long been in the making. It is a testament to what is possible through constant consistent dedicated positive action and the complete love and support of the countless friends, family, acquaintances and total strangers who have always been there for me during the hard and trying times which for a while seemed like most times. Without you there never would be a book called *The Crossover: Making Your Biggest Dreams Your Greatest Reality*. Without you my dreams may have suffocated long ago. Lord knows that I've been through a few things, that I've had my fair share of sorrow and with the God sent blessings of supportive family and friends, when things got bad and I mean really bad and I began thinking that life would swallow me whole and lay waste to all that I was; I was not destroyed, I not only survived, I thrived! It is you the reader of these words and those in my past who did all they could and more to get me where I am today and helped me make my dreams come alive, THANK YOU!

Dear friends there were many a night that I paced the floor and did not know how I was going to make it. You may be going through an experience like this now and it is during these hard times all the motivation in the world cannot help you. But you've got to lean on the power of God because he will never leave you or forsake you. I thank you God above all for helping me complete this great crossing over, for Helping me to make the invisible, appear.

After God come my parents, Maxine Smith and Joseph Glenn Smith Sr. To you I owe everything, as without you I would have nothing. I love you! The greatest heroes in my life are my mother and father who stood watch over me countless nights making sure that I had every tool, every advantage, and every opportunity that was available as best they could. Though we never had much you found a way. For that and more, I thank you! I thank you mother for every overnight shift you worked to put me through school. Thank you father for all the hours you worked, the business you created, and the sacrifices you made so that I could have just a little money for the debate tournaments that were so important to me in high school. Thank you mother and father for your continuous love and support, for every kind and encouraging word ever said when I was down and halfway out. Thank you for forgiving me for all of my mistakes, missteps and poor choices I've made. I strive each day to be a better man and though I have a great distance yet to travel in this journey I am comforted in knowing that I will forever have you and the lessons you impressed upon me instilled within my heart. Thank you. Thank you one thousand times! Forever and all of eternity thank you!

It's said that behind every great man is an even greater woman and for years and years that woman was Chrystal J. Lee. A beautiful, talented, blessing of a woman if ever there was one. My first love who I shall love always for being my friend, always believing in me, for supporting me and staying with me during the hard times. I thank you! Thank you Chrystal for believing in me as very few others did. Thank you for accepting me for who I was with all of my stubbornness and obsessive behavior. Thank you for loving me when I needed love, for caring for me when I was sick and for being my solid rock and cornerstone of support that was all I had during the stressful times when I did not know how I was going to make it. Thank you! I could write a whole new book on all the ways in which you've been there for me when I could barely be there for myself. I wont write another book on this but I will say that I have not forgotten. I have not forgotten nor will I ever forget the big little things you did to help me make this great crossover. Thank you! Thank you for being you! You are wonderful and I love you!

A critical portion of my journey took place at Wayne State College. I want to thank Wayne State College and all the wonderful staff and faculty who helped me as I made my way through the rigors of collegiate study. Wayne State College touts itself as a school where bright futures begin. They are absolutely correct in that statement! If I could describe for you in one word what Wayne State College means to me that word would be *opportunity*. The amount of opportunities available at Wayne State College is beyond measure. It was at that institution for higher learning that I had the great experiences that taught me I could in fact do what I dreamt, and that I could achieve that which I set out to achieve. To all who make this place great, past and present, who go the distance in supporting those starting their journey in life; thank you. A tremendous and huge thanks to: Dr. Shelia Stearns (thanks for giving me the chance to speak at my graduation in 2003), Dr. Joe Blankenau, Dr. Monica Snowden, Larry Emanuel, Penny Russel Roberts, Maureen Carrigg, Dr. Richard Collings, Donovan Roy, Yano Jones, Dr. Sharon Thomas, Virginia Feeley, Karen Granburg, Dr. Mark Leeper, Curt Frye, Max McElwain, Annalise Hawthorne R.I.P., all members of the Wayne Stater Staff, everyone at KWSC-TV, K-92 radio, Thank you all for helping and allowing me to be me during my time attending this great place. Wayne State College, where bright futures begin!

To my beloved siblings, who for all my 32 years of life have consistently been my fortress of support and remain so to this very day. Surely one of the great blessings God can bestow upon any of us is a great family enhanced by the love and support of great siblings. Thank you Glennesia Skipper, Tamara Brethower, Jeran Smith and William Smith ... for everything! I LOVE YALL!

I've heard over and over and over again that God puts people in our lives for a reason, a season or a lifetime. We never really know during our time with individuals which category they fall into as it's usually after a relationship ends that such a discovery is had. Each season has its own unique purpose and whatever Gods reasons for placing Crystal "Gmice" Ford in my life are I'm thankful and certainly grateful. In many ways this woman saved my life as I have told her on more than one occasion. Crystal Ford loves me and supports me dutifully as a great woman and partner should. Though we are not together, she loves and supports me still. For this, I am thankful.

This book has been a long time coming and if it wasn't for the help, support and blessings from family, friends and loved ones this book surely would not have made it from the idea stage to written and typed stage to the now printed stage and into your hands. Crystal Ford is most certainly one of those blessed loving supporters who helped me to achieve what this book is about, completing this great crossover. Only God knows what else is in store for me. Only God knows what purpose there is for the talents he has bestowed upon me but it's clear to me that no amount of greatness I had sought to achieve would have been possible without the blessings and love from others. This beautiful woman stands among those who are fabulous in their efforts to help me attain my own level of greatness. God Bless You! I Love You!

To all my friends, supporters and all others who have blessed me on my journey, Thank you! Michael Wells, Christian Appeldorn, Walter Pearson, Roni Davis and RARE Boutique and Salon, Dell Gines, Christine Swinney, Chada Mims, Pastor John Voner, Tim Collins, Patrick Taylor, Tommie Wilson, Kendal Johnson, Kenny Pearson, Heath "Beefy" Hysell, Kevin Bracy, Crystal Ford, Mack McGhee, Jeff Bridges, Robin Quarles, Gabriel Mussleman, Chrystal Lee, George "BJ" Burns Jr., Jazmine Everett, Jrome Wilson, Judd Theil, Kimara Snipes, Ambrose Lawanga, Morghan Price, Orentheian Everett, Robert Bennet, Rolisha Davis, Ryan Tweedy, Sonsylraye Carson, Tavis Pryor, Mahdiyyah Mims, Ishma-El Muhammad-Bey, Kasai Mimms, Jamael Mimms, Tim Rexius and Rexius Nutrition, Kyle Triggs of Triggs Computer Consulting, World Fellowship Christian Center, Dr. Hauser and staff at Hauser Chiropractic, Elite Good Ones, Inc., Dr. Korth and staff at Performance Chiropractic, Jeff Cox and Old Country buffet, Louis Rotella III and Rotella Italian Bakery, Kevin Neal, Pastor Ernest Sweat III, and Mt. Sinai Church of God in Christ. THANK YOU ALL SO VERY MUCH!

There are so many people who should be on this list. I apologize for missing out on those who have not come to mind at this moment but know that your support was and is needed, felt and appreciated. God Bless you all!

Biography

Born in New Orleans, Louisiana, Joseph Glenn Smith, II became a Nebraskan after moving to the state with family in 1989 seeking greater opportunities and has since lived in Arkansas and recently relocated to Maryland. It was in Nebraska; Joseph developed and cultivated a love of information, debate, personal motivation, fitness, goal attainment and global progress for human kind. The speaker, author and social engineer is a graduate of Wayne State College with a B.S. degree in journalism. Today he uses his fiery voice and commanding stage presence to advance the cause of education, human rights and political empowerment for all the worlds' people.

Joseph has a natural ability to connect with others and is especially effective at establishing and nurturing a rapport with young people. Because of his constant work with the education and political communities he has surfaced as an expert on youth, politics and social policy. He is a consultant in this area and has worked with political, educational and health care organizations to improve life in his community.

In addition, he is the founder of Global Renaissance, LLC, a company that is dedicated to changing the operational attitudes of others so that more people will be better able to recognize their talents and become contributors to global history by leaving lasting legacies of love, creativity and peace. An organization that prepares youth for global competitiveness and engagement while increasing the young minds' power and proficiency in the areas of critical thinking, conflict resolution, complex problem solving and intercultural diplomacy and negotiation. Teaching and training youth for the rigors of social engagement for the purpose of creating thoughtful and dedicated global change agents are among his great passions.

Lastly, Joseph is the team leader of the Omaha Dream Team spearheading the 1st Omaha Ambassador Trek and Arkansas Ambassador Trek, partnering with Non-Government organization BuildOn and a growing number of the businesses, organizations and the faith community. The Omaha Dream Team is an 18-member coalition of young entrepreneurs and youth all from Omaha, Nebraska and all dedicated to making a positive difference in the world at large and within their own community. They are business owners, educators, entrepreneurs, authors, students, fitness instructors, international humanitarians and more. They are leaders who yearn to show youth the path to personal achievement and success through love, service and dedications to our brothers and sisters in our collective society and will be leaving for Malawi, East Africa and Nicaragua, Central America intent to build a three-room schoolhouse.

The Ambassador Trek program is important because this venture is premised on the firm and real belief that any and all things are possible with an unwavering belief and love of God. This history-making endeavor will be made possible due to Gods help and will go far in establishing a moral code within our youth that it is a good thing to help others. It is necessary because the Malawian and Nicaraguan community will receive a school they need and in building this school the young participants will have a unique and rare opportunity otherwise not offered; an opportunity to see the world through the eyes and experiences of others thereby changing their operational attitudes, thereby allowing them to become a majestic positive influence upon their peers.

More Information can be found at GlobalRenaissanceMovement.com if interested in supporting the Ambassador Trek start by subscribing to Joseph's blog. Each free subscription brings inspirational wisdom and to your mind and serves as another blessed step in the righteous direction of dream fulfillment. Support for the businesses and organizations that have supported the Ambassador Trek is strongly encouraged. Their blessed and wonderful help has made this venture possible.

His future plans include running for political office, building more schools in more countries through future Ambassador Treks and living out Gods plan to be the greatest man he possibly can!

"I seek to educate, challenge, and enlighten others. To discuss and share ideas and perspectives on subjects of real importance, that actually makes a difference in our daily lives."

Glossary of Key Terms and Elements

Human Capital: the abilities and skills of any individual, especially those acquired through investment in education and training that enhance potential income earning.

The Great Crossover: completion of the dream fulfillment process; of making ones dreams come true, crossing from the real of intangibility to our physical realm of existence. This Great Crossover is the definitive action of an individual or society moving from grand imaginations to grand achievements, from great intentions to great actions and living the results from those actions

Participation: The fact of taking part, as in some action or attempt. Sharing as in benefits or profits.

Respect: Esteem for a sense of the worth or excellence of a person, a personal quality or ability, or something considered as a manifestation of a personal quality or ability. The condition of being esteemed or honored.

Optimism: A disposition or tendency to look on the more favorable side of events or conditions and to expect the most favorable outcome. The belief that good ultimately predominates over evil in the world.

Growth: the act or process or a manner of growing; development or gradual increase. The process of moving through stages of development. The slow process of becoming a more complex human originating as something more simple.

Responsibility: A particular burden of obligation upon one who is responsible. Reliability or dependability in meeting debts or what is otherwise owed to another.

Energy: the capacity for vigorous activity. The ability of matter to do work. Fuel and other resources used for the operation of machinery.

Support: To keep from falling or sinking. To hold in position. To give strength to, to enable to last or continue. To supply with necessaries to assist by ones approval or presence or by subscription of funds to a cause or person. To be a fan of, speak in favor of or vote for.

Spirituality: The quality or fact of being spiritual. Characterization by or suggesting predominance of the spirit of an entity or the universe pertaining to spirits or the supernatural associated in interests, attitude and outlook.

Enlightenment: a transformational intellectual awakening, characterized by belief in the power of human reason and by innovations and knowledge gained in political, religious, economic and educational doctrines.

Progress: a movement toward a goal or to a further or higher stage; advanced steady improvement as a society or civilization.

Perseverance: steady persistence in a course of action, a purpose, a state, etc., especially in spite of difficulties, obstacles, or discouragement.

Ambition: an earnest desire for some type of achievement or distinction, as power, honor, fame, or wealth, and the willingness to strive for its attainment

Epiphany: A sudden realization of great truth

Initiative: an introductory act or step; leading action: *to take the initiative in making friends.* Readiness and ability in initiating action

Prodigious*:* extraordinary in size, amount, extent, degree, force

Struggle: to contend with an adversary or opposing force. To contend resolutely with a task, problem, etc.; strive: *to struggle for existence.*

NOTES

www.ingramcontent.com/pod-product-compliance
Lightning Source LLC
Chambersburg PA
CBHW052036070526
44584CB00016B/2070